Heaven Hears Each Whisper

Answered Prayers in Everyday Life

6-27-00

Dee,
you & I are at an
unique place right
now. I'm time, we
will be stronger
having gone through
these lessons. I
love you,
Sara

Heaven Hears Each Whisper

Answered Prayers in Everyday Life

Kelsey Tyler

BERKLEY BOOKS, NEW YORK

HEAVEN HEARS EACH WHISPER

A Berkley Book / published by arrangement with
the author

PRINTING HISTORY
Berkley trade paperback edition / April 1996

The Berkley World Wide Web site address
is http: /www.berkley.com

ISBN: 0-425-15156-5

BERKLEY®
Berkley Books are published by The Berkley Publishing Group,
200 Madison Avenue, New York, New York 10016.
BERKLEY and the "B" logo
are trademarks belonging to Berkley Publishing Corporation.

PRINTED IN THE UNITED STATES OF AMERICA

10 9 8 7 6 5 4 3 2 1

Acknowledgments

For many reasons, the writing of this book came at an especially difficult time in my life. It would have been impossible to pull it together if it weren't for the constant prayers and support of my church families at West Valley Christian and Verde Valley Christian, and of course the prayers of my extended family of parents, sisters, brothers, cousins, nieces, nephews, aunts, and uncles around the country. Heaven heard and still hears your whispered prayer. Please know that I have been surrounded by God's peace and my family has been deeply encouraged amidst uncertain times. Thank you.

There are others who have helped make this book possible, and I wish to thank them also. First, the hardworking, honest people who took time from their busy lives to tell me their stories. Whispered prayer is often a private and heartfelt matter. It is my intention to treat the incidents you've shared with me delicately. I pray that others will be strengthened and encouraged with a renewed faith as they read the treasures you have so generously shared.

I want to thank, as always, my editor, Elizabeth Beier. Once again you have taken a dream, a conversation even, and turned it into a beautiful collection. Thank you for your patience and tireless effort; I am privileged to work with you.

Next, thanks to Angela Davis, who was willing to bring a toddler and a newborn to my house each day, forsaking any hope of peace and quiet while she entertained her children and mine so I could write. I couldn't have done it without you.

Arthur Pine and his hardworking crew also deserve my thanks. The vision has grown over the years, and now these stories and those of past books will be shared across the world for years to come.

And my deepest thanks to my husband and children for providing me with life's most special moments. Also thanks to Gina Hammond for providing me with the very best ideas, all of which have gone into this book. You're the best friend anyone could have. And to Sherri Reed, I am so thankful that you came into my life when you did. Without you and your own incredible answers to prayer, I might never have thought of this collection. Finally to my parents, for continuing to be my best publicists and supporters. I love you all. May this collection be a tribute to that love.

Dedicated to:

My husband, who continues to prod me
toward prayer
even when there seems to be mountains
barring the way.
You always believe that God will hear
and you smile with me
each time he does.

My children, whose innocent prayers are
offered up
with far more faith and insight
than anything a grown-up could say.

My special friends, Gina, Sherri, Christine,
Jo Ann, Amber, Lisa, and Pat.
You are always there to pray with me and
for me.
I treasure your friendship and
the common ground we share.

Wendy and Roger, Cindy and Jim,
whose long-ago prayers changed
my life forever.
As a single domino affects an endless
number of others,
so each of you have made a difference
in ways you'll never understand this side
of Heaven.

And to God, the Father, and my Lord and
Savior, Jesus Christ,
who sees each teardrop,
knows each heartache,
feels each person's pain.
Because of you,
Heaven does, indeed, hear each whisper.

Introduction

In conducting research for my previous books, *There's an Angel on Your Shoulder* and *It Must Have Been a Miracle*, I came across dozens of stories that were not entirely angel encounters nor miracle stories. Rather they were tales of everyday people whose lives were changed by answered prayer or what they believed was divine assistance. They were stories of hope where once there was none.

In some situations the answer came in five minutes or even five seconds: the superhuman strength on the part of a passerby to perform a rescue, or the uncanny occasion when someone was encouraged in the right way at the right time. In other cases, such as that of a paralyzed young woman regaining the use of her legs and walking up the aisle to marry her sweetheart, the answer took years.

I hope that you are lifted and inspired as you read the stories of people who disregarded earthly limitations and realized the truly amazing, the supernatural—because they took the time to seek it, to ask for it. And that perhaps after reading these stories you will view your world differently, stopping to ask for that which might seem utterly impossible and looking for divine answers as you make your way through life.

Perhaps then you, too, will believe that Heaven hears each whisper.

Foreword

We are living in a time when nearly everyone believes there is more to life than what we see, more than merely life and death. Look around. True stories of angel assistance delight us; accounts of miracles give us hope.

Although crime abounds, we are no longer fascinated with it as we once were. We have long since grown tired of it. And so we continue to search for a thread of hope in the tapestry of life, yearning for stories that delight rather than depress.

After years of cynicism, it is as if we have come full circle, believing as our forefathers did that God sees our pain, our desperate situation, and that he strengthens our faith by working the supernatural amidst the mundane. We have reached a place where we are willing to believe that his help may take the form of angels, of miracles, or of that most personal manifestation of all—answered prayer.

Heaven hears us and so we have hope.

We hear the story of the dying man who is comforted by a male nurse in his final hours, and we feel goose bumps when we later learn that the hospital employed no such nurse. An angel? we wonder. Our hearts soar with the possibility.

We take note of incidents in which there simply is no earthly explanation for what has happened. A miracle? we ask, and the future seems brighter.

But there are other stories, too, stories like the one about the highway patrol officer who tentatively pulls over an eighteen-wheeler on a dark, deserted desert highway. As he approaches the cab he realizes he has not radioed for backup and he hopes there will be no confrontation.

"Got a light out, back of the truck, left side," the officer states, noting that the trucker is a thousand miles from his home base. "No ticket this time. Just get it fixed."

The trucker's eyes narrow and he climbs down from the cab, staring strangely at the officer. "What'd you say?"

The officer shifts his weight uncomfortably and repeats himself.

The trucker is silent several seconds. Then he speaks. "You were in Vietnam, weren't you?" he asks, his eyes narrow, searching those of the officer.

"Yes." The officer is puzzled. "Why?"

Drifting back in time, the trucker narrates the incident clearly. His military unit was under heavy attack and he had been hit badly. The others were about to flee in a waiting helicopter and had wanted to leave him behind. But the commanding officer would not allow it. He worked over the bleeding soldier until he could be transferred to a gurney and lifted into the helicopter.

"I couldn't see you very well," the trucker says. "But I forced myself to remember your voice so that someday I could find you and thank you. I've prayed about this meeting every day since then. I begged God to let me meet you. You saved my life, and I couldn't imagine leaving this life without the chance to tell you thanks."

A trucker prays for the chance to thank the man who once saved his life. He's a thousand miles away from home when he's pulled over by the very man who rescued him. All because a tail-light was out.

Answered prayer? Can it be that God is listening if only we will ask?

We are inspired by the possibility.

Not everyone has experienced an angel encounter or been the recipient of a miracle. But according to some studies, as many as eighty percent of us believe in prayer and that our prayers have been answered. We believe because we have seen. We have received supernatural results after asking for them. We have experienced answers to our own prayers, and seen them happen in the lives of people around us.

These stories will let you imagine the "impossible." They will delight you, and may fill you with the greatest hope of all—the possibility that we are not alone, spinning hopelessly toward an empty end, but that there is someone watching over us and listening.

A Note to the Reader: In putting this collection together, I had the privilege of talking with most of the people whose answered prayers appear in detail in this book. In some instances, the names of the people involved have been changed to protect their privacy. In these cases, names are fictitious and are not intended to represent specific living persons. On the few occasions when it was impossible to contact secondary people involved, the details were provided by a person who witnessed the event in question firsthand and believed the story to be both truthful and completely credible. It is the author's opinion that God does indeed answer prayer. But at the same time it is not the author's intention to prove the validity of the answered prayers in this book. Rather they have been captured as honestly as possible for you to evaluate and judge for yourself.

ANSWER ONE:

The Jane Chain

*O*n Sunday, July 24, 1994, Kara Brenner looked at her wristwatch and saw that it was exactly twelve o'clock noon. Time to pray for Jane. She found a quiet place in her house and for the next thirty minutes—sometimes with tears in her eyes—she spoke to God in hushed tones, pleading with him to spare the life of Jane Crisp.

When thirty minutes had passed, Kara's husband, Bob, began praying. He, too, had committed himself to take a shift praying for Jane.

The hours wore on and the Jane Chain continued. Sharon Wood: 1:30 p.m. Linda Gresham: 2 p.m. Don Schooler: 2:30 p.m. Penny McCravy: 3 p.m.

Sunday evening came, and with it Chipper Brown and Jack Finley at 7 p.m. Janet Prince: 7:30 p.m. Sonia McCalley: 8 p.m.

Night turned into the wee hours of the morning and still there was constant prayer. Jim Barrow: 1:30 a.m. Kevin Williams: 2:30 a.m. Tom Wells: 5 a.m.

And so the Jane Chain continued.

All across the town of Poway, California, the people of Pomerado Christian Church kept up the Jane Chain: twenty-four hours of continuous prayer uttered in thirty-minute segments by forty-eight people who had willingly signed up earlier that morning.

Never had the church prayed so consistently and so fervently for a single life. But this was more than a normal emergency. Jane Crisp, thirty-eight, was at the Balboa Naval Hospital in San Diego fighting for every breath of life. The night before, doctors had told her husband that she was dying.

"There's nothing more we can do," one of the doctors had said. "It's between her and God now."

Prayer was the only way Jane's church family knew to help. Not just for Jane, but for her tiny newborn baby as well.

On Monday morning Laurie Franklin picked up the chain at 7 a.m. Carol Stafford: 9 a.m. Audrey Williams: 11 a.m.

These were Jane's friends, the people of Pomerado Christian. And they knew how badly the Crisps had wanted this baby. It shook them to their core to imagine her newborn son never knowing his mommy.

A few years earlier, Mike and Jane Crisp's daily prayer was always the same. They wanted another child, and they believed God would answer their prayers when the timing was perfect. They had two beautiful sons, Tom and John. But they dreamed of raising lots of children, and now Jane was having trouble getting pregnant.

Then, three years after John was born, Jane became pregnant. But what seemed like an answered prayer became instead a sorrow-filled time when Jane lost the baby in her fifth month of pregnancy.

Searching for reasons why God would allow the death of their third child, the Crisps arrived at the only conclusion they could. God was in control and he had a reason for what had happened. Not long after the miscarriage, Jane and Mike once again began asking God for another child, still believing prayer was their only hope.

Then in January 1994, Jane found out she was pregnant again.

Once more she thanked God for the life within her and asked him to protect her unborn baby.

From the beginning, Jane's body did not cooperate. During her sixth week of pregnancy doctors analyzed the results of an ultrasound test and discovered that she had placenta previa—a condition which typically corrects itself by the fourth month but which can be potentially dangerous.

"I feel great," Jane assured her husband, Mike. "I'm sure everything will be just fine."

Mike, thirty-eight, needed reassuring. He was a fighter pilot with the U.S. Navy stationed at the famous Miramar air base. Often he was gone for months at a time, flying watch missions near the Persian Gulf or in other hostile areas.

Weeks passed, and Mike was in the middle of such an operation when Jane began bleeding. At first the flow of blood was relatively light, and as she checked herself into the hospital that day, Jane's concern was only for her unborn baby. There were still more than three months left until her due date.

Within hours doctors realized that Jane's placenta had not corrected its position. Instead, it had grown through her uterine wall, causing bleeding from her uterus.

"The baby is fine," the doctor told her. "But we're keeping you here. We need to watch you very closely until we can safely deliver your baby."

Mike Crisp was in his stateroom aboard the naval carrier U.S.S. *Carl Vinson* on the afternoon of June 24 when he received Jane's call. She quickly explained the situation, trying to ease his immediate concerns.

"Honey, everything's okay," she said calmly. "I'm having a little bleeding, that's all. They're going to keep me here just in case there's a problem."

"Do you want me there?" Mike was ten thousand miles from home, but he could be back in four days if there was an emergency situation.

"No." Jane was firm. "You'll be home in six weeks anyway. If anything goes wrong, they'll call you. And in the meantime, I'm in good hands here at the naval hospital. Don't worry."

"I *am* worried," Mike said, frustrated that he was so far away.

As they spoke, the ship pushed through the waters of the Persian Gulf, beginning the long trek back to San Diego and Miramar. But that brought Mike no comfort; suddenly the days ahead seemed like an eternity.

"I wish I were with you, Jane."

"Really, Mike. I'll be fine." She paused for a moment. "But please pray for the baby. He's too little to be born yet."

Mike felt tears well up in his eyes, and he swallowed hard. "I'll be praying, sweetheart. You just hang in there until I get home."

For two weeks doctors monitored Jane's condition, checking often to see if her body was handling the problems with the placenta.

Then, on July 2, Jane began to hemorrhage. Immediately doctors rushed her into surgery and performed a cesarean section to remove the baby.

"It's a boy and he's alive," one of the doctors announced as others worked frantically about the room preparing for the surgery that would come now that the baby had been delivered. The infant was handed to neonatal specialists, cleaned, and rushed into an incubator where he was hooked up to a respirator. He weighed one pound, fourteen ounces.

For Jane, everything became a blur the moment they rushed her into surgery. She knew there was a problem and that doctors were about to do a cesarean section. But because she was bleeding so badly, they could not do a spinal block. Instead they administered a general anesthetic, and minutes before the baby was born Jane could feel herself losing consciousness.

"She's bleeding badly," she heard someone say.

"Looks like DIC." Another voice filled the room, then another, and all of it blended into a distant humming.

At that instant Jane felt a tremendous shock of pain searing through her insides as the baby was removed before the painkiller had time to take effect. She tried to talk, but her body would not respond. Instead, Jane felt herself falling, slipping further and further from consciousness. She wanted desperately to ask someone the only question that really mattered.

"Is my baby alive?" She struggled to say the words, to find the answer from one of the doctors in the room. But her lips remained motionless, and then, before she could learn the answer to her question, everything went black.

It was pitch dark—a moonless night at sea—and Mike Crisp was sleeping soundly when there was a loud rap on his stateroom door.

Groggy and unsteady, he automatically flipped his legs out of bed, stood up, and reached for the door. It was the ship's chaplain.

"Mike, I've got some bad news for you." Suddenly Mike was wide awake.

"Is it Jane?"

The chaplain nodded painfully. "We've received a call from one of the surgeons at the Balboa Naval Hospital. She began hemorrhaging and they performed an emergency C-section. The baby boy is just under two pounds. He's not going to make it."

Mike's shoulders slouched forward as he took the blow. "How's Jane?"

"Not good, Mike. She's bleeding uncontrollably," the chaplain said, placing a steady hand on Mike's shoulder. "Doctors have her in surgery right now trying to find a way to stop it. Mike, it doesn't look good for either of them."

Mike was stunned. He allowed the chaplain to pray with him, and then he sat on his bed staring at the wall. In the hours that followed, Mike remembered the fervor with which he had once prayed and loved God. He had been a youth leader at his church for three years before joining the military. Now, although he had remained morally strong, he had become distant from God.

While Jane and the boys attended church every week, he was more of a visitor, making an appearance on occasional Sundays.

There was always a good excuse why he didn't go. Fighter pilots led a busy life with a particularly demanding schedule. Many Sundays there were things he felt obligated to put before church.

He was still considering these things when the chaplain returned once more to his room, this time with better news. Jane and their newborn son had both stabilized. Still, doctors urged that he return to San Diego as quickly as possible.

That night, while Mike was waiting for a transport airplane to arrive and take him to the nearest airport in Perth, Australia, the chaplain came to his room a third time. This time with the most ominous news of all.

"They can't stop her bleeding, Mike," the chaplain said. "She's back in surgery again. The doctors are doing all they can for her. But they don't think she's going to make it. You need to hurry, Mike."

Left alone, Mike cried and prayed as he hadn't in a decade.

"Lord, take me if you have to take someone," he railed. "Our boys need Jane. She hasn't even seen her newborn son, Lord. Please, let her live."

When he arrived in Perth the next day, he was met by a friend. Immediately he telephoned the hospital in San Diego.

"She's in surgery again," he was told by a doctor. "She's still alive but she's bleeding from everywhere in her body. She has a condition called DIC—disseminated intervascular coagulation. It's the result of severe shock to the body. Her blood is not clotting as it should and so she's bleeding from all her major organs."

"What does it mean?" Mike was frantic.

"It means you need to hurry."

Mike hung up the phone, angry and frustrated. They had twelve hours before the commercial airline flight was scheduled to leave for San Diego. Then it would be more than a day in the air before he was home. His friend saw the agony in Mike's eyes, and asked if there was anything he could do to help.

"Yes," Mike said. His eyes were swollen from crying, his voice dejected. "Is there a church nearby?"

The man nodded.

"Take me there. Please."

The men drove two miles to a local church, where Mike explained the situation to the pastor.

"Just a minute," he said, picking up his telephone. "Let me make a few phone calls."

Within an hour, six men who were leaders in the church gathered in the sanctuary and formed a circle of prayer around Mike. For two hours the men prayed, imploring God to heal his wife and son and help him get home quickly. When it was time for Mike to leave for the airport, the pastor put a hand on his shoulder.

"Everyone will be praying, Mike. That is all we can do."

Mike nodded, smiling weakly through his tears. He was exhausted from the emotional and physical journey, and still there remained more than thirty hours of flying time. On the airplane Mike sat next to a man who had lost his wife a year earlier in an accident. Mike turned away and stared out the window at the endless blue sky, wondering if he would be in that man's position in a year's time.

"Lord, I can't make it without her," he prayed silently, fresh tears springing to his eyes. "Please let her live, dear God. Please."

Every moment for the rest of the flight Mike stayed in constant prayer for Jane and their baby. By the time he arrived in San Diego she was in surgery a fourth time. Mike had said more prayers in the past ninety-six hours than he had in the past decade.

In the hospital, Mike saw Pastor Evan Foote from Pomerado Christian Church.

"Evan, how is she?" he asked, hurrying into the waiting room and pulling up a chair.

"She's on a respirator, Mike. We've been praying for her and we've called everyone on the church prayer chain. But it's very, very serious."

Mike nodded, too choked up to speak. After a while he said, "I'm going to go see her."

"She doesn't look like herself," Evan warned.

Nothing could have prepared Mike for the way Jane looked. She had tubing running in and out of various areas on her face and upper body, and she was bloated from the blood and other fluids being pumped into her. Her skin was gray and lifeless. Mike remained frozen in place, working up the courage to go near her.

"Honey," he whispered, finally, inching toward her as if she would break if he moved too quickly. "It's me. Everything's going to be okay. God's gonna help you, Jane. We're all praying for you and the baby."

He stood there a few minutes more, holding her limp hand and begging God to be merciful with her life. Then, when he could not stand another minute, he left her room and went searching for his son. Again he was unprepared for what he found.

The child was so small he looked lost in the neonatal intensive care incubator, swimming in a sea of wires and monitors. His fingers were frail, no thicker than matchsticks.

"He's doing all right," the nurse whispered with a smile. "Your pastor prayed over him the first day he was born. Everything's been very stable ever since then."

Mike's lips turned upward in a partial grin as he considered the nurse's words. Prayer, again. The same prayer he'd said so little of in the last ten years. He gazed at his son, his lungs not yet developed, struggling against the odds to survive, and he made a decision. If prayer was what it would take to heal his wife and son, then he would see to it that as many people as possible were praying for them.

"God's going to take care of you, son," he whispered, still looking at the infant. He thought about the small church in Australia. "We'll have people praying for you across this whole world."

The phone calls began almost immediately.

Mike contacted friends in Florida and Ohio and asked them to pray.

"And please have your church pray for them," he'd tell the people he spoke with. "Ask them to call people they know and then have their churches start praying. Please. We need everyone praying."

The prayer chain grew. Arizona. Iowa. Military bases across the country. By that night, thousands of people were praying for Jane and their newborn baby. The prayers being said for them were so many that Mike was not surprised that evening when doctors finally were able to stop Jane's bleeding. In the past four days she'd been transfused with more than one hundred units of blood.

"Everything is not as good as it seems," the doctor told Mike. "She's lost so much blood, there's a strong possibility she'll have brain damage. Also, many of her organ functions have shut down. Everything except her heart and her brain at this point."

"Okay, so how long will it be before she can be out of here?" Mike said.

The doctor stared blankly at Mike. "What I'm saying is that she has less than a one percent chance of living. If she does live, she could be brain-damaged. She could be bedridden the rest of her life."

Mike was silent, soaking in the news. His entire life had changed in less than a week, but even as the doctor waited for him to react, he began praying again, silently asking God to heal his wife. The doctor cleared his throat and continued.

"Another thing, Mike. She's going to need a lot more blood. Maybe you could put a call in to the base and see if some of the guys might be willing to donate."

Mike made the call that night, and within two days there were more than four hundred units of blood in Jane's account. At least the blood problem was solved.

"What else can we do?" one of the guys from Miramar asked Mike. "We feel so helpless out here."

"Pray," Mike said simply. He had never been one to openly discuss his faith. But now he found it the most natural thing in the world. The doctors were taking care of Jane's physical needs. The others needed to pray.

For the next ten days Mike and Jane's mother alternated taking twelve-hour shifts with Jane and then back at home with the boys. Although she did not regain consciousness during that time, Jane made a steady recovery.

Then, almost three weeks after the baby's birth, Jane's condition suddenly took a drastic turn for the worse. Once again she began bleeding uncontrollably throughout her body. Because her organs were already weak, her stomach ruptured, forcing doctors to perform emergency surgery. They removed more than half of Jane's stomach and attempted to close off the areas where she was bleeding. She survived surgery, but doctors gave her almost no chance to live.

"It's miraculous that she's made it this far, Mike, but the truth is very clear. She's dying," the doctor said when the surgery was done. "You'll need to tell the boys."

The next morning, Mike pulled the boys close to him and told them that their mother was expected to die. With tears in their innocent eyes, the boys immediately joined hands with their father and prayed that God would let their mommy live.

Despite the gravity of Jane's condition, doctors allowed Tom, eight, and John, six, to visit their mother in the intensive-care unit that day. At one point Jane's eyes opened, but she did not respond to her boys' presence in the room. That evening after the children had gone home, Jane's fever soared to more than 105 degrees. Doctors braced for the inevitable, but Jane clung to life throughout the night as Mike and Pastor Evan Foote prayed continuously in the waiting room.

The next day, Sunday, was Jane's birthday. Evan and Mike knew that most likely it would also be the day she died. The pastor left Mike early in the morning and reported to church, where he was scheduled to preach at 8:45 that morning.

"I've been thinking about Jane Crisp," he told the congregation. "How today is her birthday and yet she lies dying in a hospital bed having never seen her newborn son and with two other sons waiting at home for her," he said. His voice was shaky, and the lack of sleep was evident in his eyes. "I know we're praying for her, but I'm not sure we're doing everything we can to call on God's divine assistance."

Evan held up a sheet of paper which read "The Jane Chain" across the top. "So today, we are going to organize. I'll be passing this sheet around and asking you to sign up, committing to pray for Jane Crisp for thirty minutes sometime in the next twenty-four hours."

There was a rustling as people reached for pens and pencils, and Evan started the sheet in the first pew.

As the sheet quickly filled with the names of volunteers, Evan returned to the pulpit. There were tears in his eyes and his voice was uncharacteristically shaky.

"At least now we can say we've done everything we know to do."

Later, when Kara Brenner began praying at noon, it was the start of one full day of continuous prayer for Jane. Even as the people prayed, Jane's mother called Mike from the hospital the next morning.

"Mike, get down here right away. Please, hurry."

Jane's father stayed with the boys, and Mike ran for his car, racing toward the hospital twenty-five miles away. He'd recognized the tone of his mother-in-law's voice. Jane was dying, despite everything. As he drove, he cried as he had never cried before. He begged and pleaded that God do whatever was necessary to let Jane live. It was the single lowest moment of his life.

Meanwhile, somewhere in Poway, Carol Stafford was praying the 9 a.m. shift—tearfully asking God to work a miracle. In Australia, the elders of the small church gathered again to take turns praying for Jane. In Arizona the people of a small rural church received word about Jane and put her on their weekly prayer chain. And across the world, fighter pilots were gearing up for the day and praying silently as they worked.

Mike sped on, unaware of the prayers being said for his wife even at that moment. Then, a few miles from the hospital, the cloud of doom that had engulfed Mike since Jane's nightmare first started suddenly disappeared. Instead, Mike felt surrounded with an unearthly feeling of peace. Although he could not explain why, at that moment he felt certain that Jane was going to survive.

When he arrived at the hospital, he was met by Jane's mother, the hospital chaplain, and a group of Jane's doctors. They ushered him into a conference room and explained the situation.

"Things have gone from bad to worse," one of the doctors said. "We'll need to do exploratory surgery to see why she's still bleeding. We may need to remove her kidney, her spleen, and her bladder. Perhaps a part of her lung."

Mike pictured the quality of Jane's life if those organs were removed. Calmly he shook his head and told the doctors they did not have permission to do that type of surgery.

"She's dying, Mike," one of them said. "We're at the end of our limit and only emergency surgery will show us what's causing the fever and infections and blood loss throughout her body." He was silent a moment, studying the faces of the others in the room. "I guarantee you if we don't do this surgery, she'll be dead in a day or two."

Finally, Mike agreed on the condition that the doctors did not remove any organ that still showed any signs of vitality. Several doctors hurried to prepare for Jane's seventh operation in three weeks. Mike was left alone with his mother-in-law and the hollow sound of their mingled sniffling.

"She's going to be all right," Mike assured her. "The prayers are working. God is healing her."

Jane's mother studied Mike. "I sure hope so; she can't stand much more of this."

Hours later doctors returned and met Mike and Jane's mother in the waiting room with Pastor Evan.

"It's absolutely incredible," one of the doctors said. "We opened her up and everything seems to be healing. There was only minimal infection and no sign of excessive bleeding."

Mike grinned broadly. "What'd I tell you?" he said, accepting a hug from his mother-in-law.

"It's still touch and go, Mike," the doctor warned.

Mike smiled, certain that the doctor thought he was losing his grip. "That's all right, Doc, because from here on out God's the one who's going to do the healing. The Jane Chain is praying for her, and I know God hears us."

Indeed, at Pomerado Christian Church, the people responsible for the Jane Chain had not heard anything about her condition. So instead of stopping, they continued the round-the-clock prayer for thirty-six hours.

As they finished, just after midnight, Jane's fever broke for the first time in days. Four days later she was conscious enough to recognize Mike and the children.

"Mike?" she asked, her eyelids heavy and her words slurred. He was at her side in a flash.

"Honey, thank God you're awake. We've been so terribly worried about you, Jane. Everyone's praying."

"The baby . . ." Her voice trailed off in fear. "Is . . . is he dead?"

"No, honey, he's just fine. He's a little guy, but he's in an incubator and he's coming along great."

"Oh, Mike, I thought he was dead!" She began to cry silently, and Mike rubbed her feet. They had started to curl from the atrophy taking place in her muscles, and Mike was determined to help her regain her strength.

A week later they wheeled Jane into the neonatal intensive-care unit to see David Michael Crisp for the first time. There was not a dry eye in the room as the nurses who had been caring for David for more than a month watched while Jane first peered at her son.

Jane smiled at the baby with all the love a mother could muster.

"I love you, little David," she said.

"The two of you are living answers to prayer," Mike piped in. "Wait till he's old enough to understand what a miracle he is."

There were more tears then, until finally one of the nurses broke in.

"Listen, Mrs. Crisp, you better work on getting yourself strong again; otherwise that little guy's going to beat you home."

Everyone laughed, and Mike nodded, taking the cue and wheeling Jane back to her room.

On September 2, two months after David's birth, Jane Crisp came home from the hospital. Along her cul-de-sac every neighbor had hung out welcome-home banners and balloons.

"They knew you weren't supposed to have visitors," Mike explained, enjoying the look of surprise on his wife's face. "But they wanted you to know that in addition to everyone else who's been praying, they have been, too."

Jane was speechless, overwhelmed by the outpouring of prayer and love she had received since David's birth. The best was yet to come: Exactly one week later, David came home.

For the next six months Jane's mother served as the infant's primary caretaker while Jane continued to recover. In all, she had received more than two hundred units of blood, lost her reproductive organs and most of her stomach, and suffered through seven operations in a three-week period.

The incident changed Mike's life.

"I don't care if I'm pumping gas or flying F-14s," he said. "The only thing that really matters in life is my faith and my family."

Doctors at the Balboa Naval Hospital told Mike and Jane that they will always talk about her miraculous recovery.

"She had that Jane Chain almost literally hanging on her bed," one of them said later. "People were praying for that young mother around the clock. Then she does the impossible and pulls out of a definitely fatal situation. I have no medical explanation for why Jane Crisp is alive today."

But the people on the Jane Chain do.

"God heard the prayers of the people and he answered them," Evan Foote said. "Plain and simple."

An Answer at the Truck Stop

*D*avid Hunter received the call just after nine on a Saturday evening in 1986 while on patrol with the sheriff's department in Knox County, Tennessee. A woman was weeping loudly in a corner booth at the Raccoon Valley Truck Stop. Several patrons had grown concerned and contacted the sheriff's department.

Hunter sighed and turned his patrol car in the direction of the truck stop. As a veteran officer of eight years, he had seen so much pain in the lives of people that he could only imagine what might cause a woman to weep aloud in a truck stop.

As he drove the remaining three miles, he remembered how pain was the reason he had joined the police force in the first place. He had ridden along with a police officer one night as part of the research he'd had to do for a local newspaper story he was writing.

The first call of the night involved a woman who

had been badly beaten by her husband. Hunter watched as the officer handcuffed the man and led him away; he saw the relief in the woman's face, and suddenly something clicked. He might write a thousand stories about good and evil in the course of a lifetime. But none of them could do for that woman what the police officer had just done. No story could rescue her from her pain.

Hunter began seeking police work the next day, and never once looked back. Now, eight years later, his love of his work was just as strong as it had been in the beginning. Despite the danger and frustration that came with the job, there were always nights like that one in which he could still make a difference for someone in pain.

Not sure what he would find, Hunter entered the truck stop cafe and immediately spotted the woman, still weeping, her face covered with her hands. Nearby sat two frightened little blond girls, ages about four and five.

Hunter's face softened as he approached the children.

"What seems to be the matter, girls?" he asked them. The older child turned to look at him, and Hunter could see she had tears in her eyes, too.

"Daddy left us," she said. "He put our stuff out of the car while we was in the bathroom."

Hunter's heart sank. He studied the woman, and gently placed a hand on her shoulder. Then he looked at the girls and smiled a warm, comforting smile. "Well, now, is that so?"

The children nodded.

"In that case I want you two to climb on those stools over there and order something to eat."

Reluctantly the girls walked away from their mother and took separate stools along the counter. Hunter signaled the waitress and asked her to get the girls whatever they wanted from the menu.

With the children out of earshot, the officer sat down across from the woman. She looked up from her hands and stared sadly at Hunter, her eyes filled with heartbreak.

"What's the problem?" Hunter asked quietly.

"Just what my girl said," the woman replied, wiping her eyes. "My husband's not cruel. Just at the end of his rope. We're flat broke, and he figured we'd get more help alone than if he stayed. I've been sitting here praying about what to do next, but I don't even have the money for a phone call. I just want to know God is listening, you know?"

Hunter nodded, his eyes gentle and empathetic. And silently he added his own prayer, asking God to show him a way to help this woman and her little children. He touched the gold St. Michael medallion he always wore around his neck. Although most police officers didn't spend a great deal of time talking about religion, Hunter knew few who did not rely on their faith. Many officers wore the St. Michael medallion under their uniforms because the archangel was recognized as the patron saint of warriors. Hunter believed with all his heart that God had indeed used angels to protect him in the line of duty on more than one occasion.

She needs an angel about now, Lord, he prayed silently. *Please help her out.*

Hunter broke the silence between the woman and him. "Do you have family?"

"The nearest is in Chicago."

Hunter thought a moment, and then suggested several agencies that could help her. As they spoke, the waitress brought hot dogs and french fries to the children, and the officer stood up and moved toward the counter. He took out his wallet to pay the bill.

"The boss says no charge," the waitress said. "We know what's going on here."

Hunter smiled at the woman and nodded his thanks. Then he stooped down to ask the girls how they liked their food. As he did, a trucker stood up from his table and approached the waitress. He mumbled something to her, and then she took him by the arm and led him to Hunter.

It was unusual for a truck driver to approach Hunter on his own. Typically truck drivers and police officers had something of a natural animosity for each other. Most truck drivers tended to see the police as cutting into their earnings by writing them tickets, while the police saw truckers as reckless people who placed their potential earnings before safety. The truth, of course, was somewhere in the middle, but still, Hunter couldn't remember a time when he'd been approached by a truck driver outside of the line of duty.

The trucker wore jeans, a T-shirt, and a baseball cap. He walked up to the counter and stood alongside Hunter. The officer noticed that the normal buzz of conversation and activity had stilled and the cafe was silent. Most of the patrons—nearly all of them long-distance truckers—were watching the conversation between the trucker and the officer.

"Excuse me, officer," the man said. "Here."

The trucker reached out his hand and gave the officer a fistful of bills. He cleared his throat.

"We passed the hat. There ought to be enough to get the woman and her girls started on their way."

Back when he was a boy Hunter had learned that cops don't cry, at least not in public. So he stood there, speechless until the lump in his throat disappeared and he was able to speak.

Then Hunter shook the man's hand firmly. "I'm sure she'll appreciate it," he said, his voice gruff from covering up his emotion. "Can I tell her your name?"

The trucker raised his hands and backed away from the officer. "Nope. Just tell her it was from folks with families of their own."

Hunter nodded, and thought of the fiercely loyal way in which people in Tennessee looked out for each other. When the trucker walked away, Hunter counted the money and was again amazed. A small room of truck drivers had in a matter of minutes raised two hundred dollars, enough money for three bus tickets to Chicago and food along the way.

The officer walked back to the booth and handed the money to the woman, at which point she began to sob again.

"He heard," she whispered through her tears.

"Ma'am?" Hunter looked confused, wondering who the woman was talking about.

"Don't you see?" she said. "I came here completely desperate, hopeless. And I sat in this booth and asked God to help us, to give us a sign that he still loved us and cared for us."

Hunter felt chills along his arms and remembered his own prayer, how he had asked God to send help and provide this woman with angelic assistance. The truck drivers certainly didn't look like a textbook group of angels, but God had used them all the same. "You know, ma'am, I think you're right. I think he really did hear."

At that instant, a young couple entered the truck stop, saw the sobbing woman, and approached her without hesitating. They introduced themselves and asked if they could help in any way.

"Well," the woman said, "I could use a ride to the bus stop. See I've got the money now and I need to get to . . ."

Hunter stood up and walked discreetly away from the scene to a quiet corner of the truck stop, where he radioed dispatch.

"The situation's resolved," he said.

Then he walked toward his patrol car and climbed inside. When he was safely out of sight he let the tears come, tears that assured him he would never forget what happened that night in the truck stop. As a patrol officer he had almost always seen the worst in people around him. But that night, he'd been reminded that kindness and love do exist among men. And Hunter had learned something else. Sometimes God answers prayer by using nothing more than a dozen big-hearted truckers sharing coffee at a truck stop in East Tennessee—and playing the part of angels.

Someone to Guide Him

*T*hree-year-old Randy Scogin marched across the yard and toward the back door of his family's house in Houston, Texas. He pulled a toy dog on wheels behind him. The air was particularly humid that Sunday afternoon in June 1975, and the child found his mother inside talking on the telephone to her sister. She glanced at the boy and he waved, his brown eyes sparkling with adventure.

"Bye, Mommy," he said. "I'm going to Bo-Bo's house."

Marilyn, twenty-nine, smiled at the child. "Okay, Randy, have fun."

Bo-Bo, the children's grandmother, lived five miles away, and Marilyn knew Randy would never really consider such a thing. The boy was playing a game of make-believe, as he had so many other times, and Marilyn felt at ease as she continued her conversation and watched the child disappear into the backyard.

Fifteen minutes later Marilyn hung up the telephone and sauntered outside to round up Randy and his six-year-old brother, Rusty. The older child was sitting in a frustrated heap, having given up his attempt to fly a kite on such a still summer day. The temperature was rising, and Marilyn wanted the children to come inside before they were affected by the heat.

"No wind, huh?" she said, bending over and fingering the limp kite.

Rusty shook his head and sighed.

"Well, it's getting too hot out here. Let's go inside and have some cold lemonade." She stood up and glanced around the yard. "Where's Randy?"

Rusty gathered his kite and shrugged as he struggled to his feet. "He was pulling that little dog, but he's been gone for a while."

"Rusty, go ask the neighbors if they've seen him." Marilyn took the kite from her oldest son, and the boy set off running. "Hurry back!" she shouted.

Marilyn flew across the yard into the house and fought back a wave of panic. Certainly the child was in the house, perhaps taking a nap with the boys' father. But inside, Marilyn searched closets and bedrooms, and finally found Harold sleeping alone.

"Harold, wake up!" she said, her voice frantic. "Randy's missing."

Harold's eyes flew open, and together he and Marilyn searched the house and yard again. Rusty returned from checking with the neighbors and announced that no one had seen Randy that afternoon.

"What's the last thing you remember him saying or doing?" Harold asked, fully awake and filled with concern.

Marilyn ran her fingers nervously through her hair. "I was on the phone with my sister and Randy told me he was going to Bo-Bo's house. I thought he was just playing and I said okay."

Marilyn and Harold exchanged a sickening look. Thirty minutes had passed since Randy's disappearance. If their son had attempted the five-mile walk to his grandmother's house by himself, he could have been kidnapped or hit by a car. Most frightening of all, he could be anywhere at all because the child was too young to have any sense of direction.

Immediately Marilyn ran to the telephone and called her mother.

"Randy's lost," she said breathlessly, closing her eyes and forcing herself to concentrate. "He left here half an hour ago and he said he was going to your house."

Five miles away, the older woman's face turned white. "He'll never make it! Even if he knows the way, there's two busy streets between your house and mine," she murmured. "Marilyn, stay there. I'll leave right now and check every street on the way. Don't worry, we'll find him or I'll know the reason why."

"Thanks, Mom." There were tears in Marilyn's eyes as she handed the telephone to Harold. She felt rooted to the spot as she watched him frantically dial the local police station.

"Our little boy wandered off and we can't find him anywhere. We think he might be trying to find his grandmother's house." Harold gripped the receiver tightly and waited while the station operator connected him with a police officer.

"What's your child look like, sir?" the officer asked.

"He's three years old, about two-and-a-half feet tall, light brown curly hair, dimples, and dark brown eyes. He's wearing a green and yellow sunsuit with brown sandals and green sunglasses. He's pulling a toy dog behind him."

As Harold spoke, Marilyn could no longer stand still. Every moment that passed meant that Randy could be getting run over or picked up by a stranger. She struggled to breathe, suffocated by the feeling of helplessness.

On the verge of hysteria, she grabbed the car keys. "I'll be back!" she shouted as she ran out the door and climbed into their family sedan.

Covering her face with her hands, she began to pray. "Please,

God. Please watch over Randy and lead me to him." Then she started the car and set out to find him.

Marilyn and Harold were deeply faithful Christians and had been all their lives. Together they had taught their boys to pray and trust God in any situation where they felt they needed help. But a few months before, Marilyn's father died of cancer, and since then she had felt none of the joy that usually accompanied her faith. She had even tried letting go of her sorrow by counting her blessings, but she was still left feeling sad and empty.

Now, as she raced through the streets in her neighborhood, she was keenly aware of how precious life was and how desperately she wanted to find her son and hold him close again. She circled the block surrounding her house and branched out into the Spring Shadows Subdivision, driving up one street and down another. But there was no sign of Randy.

"Please, God," she whispered aloud. "Please take care of him and lead me to him."

Suddenly the cloud of sorrow lifted and she knew how very blessed she was, the mother of two beautiful children and married to a loving, faithful man who cherished her and the boys. If only she could find Randy, Marilyn knew she would never take these— God's greatest blessings—for granted again.

Marilyn continued to search intently along dozens of streets, but when fifteen minutes passed she decided to return home for an update. Perhaps Randy had come home or maybe the police knew something. She swerved into the driveway and saw that her mother still had not arrived. Racing inside, she found Harold and Rusty waiting by the telephone.

"The police know nothing." Harold's voice was wracked with hysteria and his eyes were filled with tears. "They can't file a missing person's report until Randy's been missing twenty-four hours."

"Isn't there anything they can do?" Marilyn's voice rose anxiously.

"They said they'll look for him and call us if they get any news."

Harold hung his head and began crying. "Not Randy," he shouted through his tears. "Not my Randy!"

At that instant Marilyn's mother arrived, and ran into the house wide-eyed. "Have you found him yet?"

"No." Marilyn turned and headed for the door with her mother in tow. "Listen, I can't just sit here, Harold. I'm getting in that car and I'm not coming back until we find our baby."

Howard wiped his eyes and clutched his oldest boy closer to him. "You go; I'll stay here with Rusty. Check back once in a while."

"Pray, Mother," Marilyn implored as she hurried across the yard toward the driver's door of the car. "Please pray."

Together the women set out along the same streets they'd already searched, working their way out from the Scogin house in every possible direction. As they drove they prayed aloud.

"Please lead us to him and please, God, please protect him." Marilyn's tears streamed down her face. "Please, God," she added, her voice barely a whisper. "He's only three years old."

Terrible thoughts filled their heads as they continued to search: Randy lying in a gutter covered with blood, or miles away in the car of some evil stranger. Marilyn knew that wherever he was, the child was scared and probably crying for her and Harold. The thought made the search unbearable, yet Marilyn had no choice but to continue.

Nearly two hours after the boy had disappeared and more than a mile from their house, the women turned onto a busy street and saw a threesome on the sidewalk half a block ahead. A tall, slim, dark-haired woman and a younger, blond woman were walking together a few feet behind a boy with curly hair wearing a green and yellow sunsuit. The child was pulling a dog behind him.

"Randy!" Marilyn screamed, and sped up, pulling alongside the trio and quickly parking her car. "My sweet Randy. Thank you, God. Thank you."

"Randy!" Marilyn shouted toward the threesome as she stepped out of the car. The women and the little boy stopped and watched as Marilyn and her mother ran toward them. Relieved and sobbing, Marilyn fell to her knees next to Randy and pulled him tightly to her, stroking his hair and closing her eyes.

"Randy, oh, Randy," she cried into his curly hair. "Thank you, God."

"Hi, Mommy. Hi, Bo-Bo!" Randy smiled easily, calm and unaffected by his adventure away from home.

Standing back, careful not to interrupt the reunion, the women who had been trailing behind the boy smiled.

"He's okay, ma'am," the older woman said softly. "He fell into a ditch back there a ways. There was a bit of water in it and we helped him out. We've been following him ever since so he wouldn't get hurt."

Marilyn nodded, still clinging tightly to the child. "Thank you so much," she said, wiping at her tears and looking Randy over to be sure he was all right.

The woman continued. "He said he lived in the shadows."

Marilyn uttered a short laugh and sniffled loudly. She and Harold had recently been trying to teach Randy his address and that he lived in the Spring Shadows Subdivision, but all that had stuck with the boy was the word "shadows."

"Anyway," the woman said, "he seemed to know where he was going."

Marilyn nodded, paying little attention to the women. All she could think of was Harold and how desperately he needed to know that Randy was safe. She swept the boy into her arms and thanked the women once more for their help. Then, fresh tears of relief streaming down her cheeks, she and her mother raced home to share the good news with the others.

Back at the house Marilyn ran inside with Randy in her arms and passed him to his crying father. "We found him walking a mile from here. Two women were walking behind him, watching out for him."

"Oh, thank you, dear Lord. Thank you," Harold said, his body flooded with relief as he hugged the boy close.

At that instant Marilyn realized something.

"Mother, we forgot to offer those women a ride home. They followed Randy all that way and I'm sure they have a long walk ahead of them." She grabbed her keys once more. "Come on, let's go find them."

Leaving Randy with his father and brother, Marilyn and her mother got into the car and returned to the spot where only minutes earlier they'd found Randy. When they turned onto the street Marilyn checked her watch. Only about four minutes had passed since they had left the women, but now as Marilyn looked up the street, there was no one in sight. As it was a long stretch of roadway without any cross streets, Marilyn was confused.

"That's strange," she muttered aloud. "No one could walk that fast. I wonder where they went."

Her mother was puzzled, too. "Let's keep looking," she said. "Maybe if we drive the length of the street we'll find them resting somewhere."

For nearly fifteen minutes Marilyn and her mother drove back and forth on the street looking carefully for the women who had so kindly watched over Randy.

"I feel so badly," Marilyn said. "They were so nice to look after Randy and then I didn't even offer them a ride home."

"Oh well," her mother finally said. "I guess they got home some other way."

There was silence for a moment.

"Mother," Marilyn said, her voice suddenly curious. "You don't think they might have been angels, do you?"

"Oh, Marilyn, come now. They were just friendly neighbors doing a kind deed."

"You're right," Marilyn said, turning the car back toward home. "Well, whoever they were, they were an answer to our prayers, that's for sure."

Back home, Marilyn hugged Randy close once more and tousled his hair. Rusty and Harold and Marilyn's mother gathered around the boy so that the family formed a circle.

"We were worried about you, Randy," Marilyn said softly.

"I know, Mommy. I won't walk off anymore."

"That's good," Harold said.

Marilyn smiled and took the boy's hands in hers. "Listen, Randy, remember those ladies who helped you and stayed with you?"

The child nodded. "Yes, Mommy. They were strangers."

"But you weren't afraid of them, were you?"

"No, they were nice."

Harold nodded. "Yes, they looked after you. Did they tell you their names?"

"They told me they were from God," Randy said simply.

There was a pause as his family leaned closer, curious expressions on their faces.

Randy looked up at his mother. "What's an angel, Mommy?"

The adults stared at the child for a moment, and then exchanged a knowing look as goose bumps rose up on each of their arms. Quietly, and with a greater understanding than at any time in his life, Harold directed his family to form a circle and hold hands; then he closed his eyes and bowed his head. When he spoke his voice was filled with awe.

"Dear God, we do not know your ways and we do not pretend to have the answers. But somehow today we know that you brought about divine intervention in the life of our little Randy. Thank you for hearing our prayers and bringing him home safely."

"God." Harold paused, his voice choked with emotion. "Thank you for the simple faith of our children. And thank you for your angels. In Jesus' name, amen."

Spared from the Fire

*C*hauncey and Betty Fairchild returned home from church one hot August Sunday in 1982 and flung open the windows of their Reno, Nevada, home. In the distance thunder rumbled and an occasional lightning bolt struck the brush-covered hills.

"It's gonna be a hot one," Chauncey predicted. "Hot and humid."

Betty wrinkled her brow and gazed out her kitchen window. Suddenly she saw smoke in the distance across the valley.

"Hey, Chauncey, come take a look at this," she said. "Looks like a brush fire over in the hills. It's not far from the Stevenson place."

Chauncey joined Betty at the window and frowned. Joe and Janice Stevenson lived three miles away on a hill overlooking the town of Reno. Behind their home was more than twenty thousand acres of brittle brush. Chauncey thought of the humidity.

"Must've been the lightning. Maybe it'll fizzle out," he suggested. "Might be too humid to amount to much."

But just an hour later the fire was roaring across the mountain range, changing directions every time the wind shifted. The Fairchilds found a pair of binoculars and watched the brittle scrub brush burn. By then, helicopters circled over the blaze dumping water and chemicals to halt the fire's progress, while firefighters worked around the perimeter with hoses.

Suddenly the Fairchilds saw the wind change direction again, this time sending the blazing fire storm directly toward the Stevensons' home. The fire was moving quickly, destroying everything in its path. Betty estimated that it would probably take no more than five minutes before it was at the edge of the Stevensons' property.

She was struck instantly by an idea.

"Chauncey, we need to pray right now for Joe's safety and for his house," she said.

Chauncey nodded. "Boys," he shouted. "Come here, please."

From the other room the Fairchilds' three sons and a neighborhood boy visiting for the afternoon joined Chauncey and Betty in the kitchen.

"Yeah?" The boys stood still, waiting to hear what was wanted of them.

"Boys," Betty explained, "the mountains are on fire and Mr. and Mrs. Stevenson's house is right in the way. We need to pray right now so that nothing happens to them or to their house."

Praying was nothing new or unusual for the Fairchild children. Their family attended the Mount Rose Evangelical Free Church— the same church to which the Stevenson family belonged—and they had grown up believing in the power of prayer. They often formed a circle so the entire family could pray together.

At Betty's suggestion, the group instantly linked hands and formed a circle in the kitchen.

"Lord and Savior," Chauncey began, "we lift up to you Joe Stevenson and his family and ask that you put a ring of protective angels around his home right now. Fire is moving too close, Dear God, and it's threatening to consume everything Joe has. We ask you in the name of Jesus to protect that home and let the fire pass by. Amen."

The others took turns praying aloud until nearly everyone had prayed. Then, after the boys had resumed their playing in the next room, the Fairchilds peered once more toward the fiery hills. This time the smoke was too thick to tell what was going on, and Betty stared nervously through her binoculars.

"Don't worry about it, Betty," Chauncey said, putting an arm around his wife's shoulders. "We've prayed about it. Now let's let God take care of the rest."

The day had started out as a busy one for Joe Stevenson. His wife and their children had set off for a visit at Janice's sister's house in Las Vegas, leaving Joe home by himself for what figured to be a lonely but peaceful week of solitude.

As the morning wore on, Joe left home for church, where he taught a discussion group on 1 Corinthians of the New Testament. Just before lunch he returned home, and as he pulled in the drive he gazed with pride, as he so often did, at his home on the hillside. The house had been ten years in the planning, and had taken another two to build. The Stevensons planned to stay there a lifetime. Joe went inside and began making plans for the afternoon.

About two hours later, he smelled smoke and looked out his window. A few miles in the distance a brush fire had started up along the mountain range adjacent to his home. *Must have been a lightning strike,* Joe thought. He went outside to watch the fire's progress, and was joined by his neighbor, Tony.

That afternoon the wind began to blow from the south, pushing the blaze farther away. Although he and Tony were concerned because of the dry brush that surrounded their homes, they felt certain that firefighters would contain the blaze before it got out of control.

"I'm going to load a few things into the car," Joe said, heading back into his house. "You never know about these firestorms."

"Okay," Tony said. "See you later. I think I'll get up on the roof and wet it down with the hose."

Joe gathered some old pictures and other irreplaceable items and packed them into his Omni. Then he, too, found his hose and began hosing down his newly finished deck. Occasionally he would spray water toward the roof, but since he had no ladder that would reach it, he could not climb on top and saturate it as he would've liked to.

Several times during the next ten minutes, church friends called to say they were praying for Joe. The knowledge that he wasn't the only one praying for protection reassured him as he returned outside after the third phone call.

But just at that moment, the wind changed directions and sent the fire directly toward Joe's house. Almost immediately, Tony came racing back to Joe's house. Together the men stood, trance-like, as they stared in horror at the inferno approaching them. Only minutes earlier the fire had seemed small and controllable. Now it was a towering wall of flames some thirty feet high, consuming everything in its path and gaining strength.

"We're in big trouble, Joe," Tony muttered, gripped with fear.

Each second the firestorm moved closer, drawing oxygen into its infernal flames and spawning whirlwinds of fire that shot fifty feet into the thick smoke above. The men watched, holding their hoses lamely as the ferocious blaze leapt over a gorge and then began moving up the hillside where their homes stood directly in its path.

Then the men snapped into action, and Joe ran to his front door, screaming for his dog. When she didn't appear at once, Joe suddenly knew he had no time to search for her.

"Come on!" Tony screamed at him. "Run for your life!"

Joe dropped his hose on the ground and the two men began running. Joe prayed aloud as he raced.

"Lord, I put my house and everything in it into your hands."

Then, still running as fast as he could, Joe remembered a passage from his discussion group earlier that day. The words of St. Paul in 1 Corinthians had stressed the importance of being thankful for everything, regardless of the outcome. Reluctantly, Joe added one more line to his prayer as he continued to run down his driveway toward his car.

"Lord, no matter what happens, I thank you for it and I praise you for who you are."

Joe jumped into his Omni, while Tony climbed into the Stevensons' other car; in seconds the two men were speeding away from the fire toward Tony's house half a mile away. There they picked up Tony's wife, warned another family in a nearby house, and continued their race for safety.

Because the lower roads were blocked by emergency vehicles, firefighters led the group of terrified homeowners up the hill toward the highway that led over the mountains to Lake Tahoe.

When he was a safe distance away from the fire and could still see the area where his home nestled, Joe stopped his car and stepped out. Other homeowners fleeing the mountainside did the same. They peered intently toward where their homes lay, but all they could see was a fog of flames and smoke where the structures should have been.

For a moment Joe was nearly overcome by what he knew was happening behind the curtain of dense smoke. In a matter of seconds, the home he and his family had planned and dreamed about for twelve years, along with a lifetime of belongings and memorabilia, was being consumed in an angry inferno.

He felt helpless, not sure whether he should scream or swear or cry. Around him others who had been evacuated from their homes were doing all of those things.

But despite Joe's sorrow and helplessness, he remained at peace, with one thought in the forefront of his mind. He was a Christian. And now, when things were worse than they'd ever been, his heart gave him no choice but to act like one.

At that instant another Bible verse came to mind: "All things work together for good to those who love God," Romans 8:28. Joe closed his eyes and forced himself to believe that promise. Then, instead of cursing God or shouting out in anger, Joe raised his voice above the roar of the fire below and praised God for all his goodness.

Joe was aware of the strange looks his neighbors were giving him, but he didn't care. With everything disintegrating in flames before his eyes, he was determined that his faith would be the single thing that was absolutely not going to be destroyed that afternoon.

For ten minutes the group of neighbors huddled in a cluster and watched as one home after another ignited in a burst of flames. The fire was moving closer, creeping along the highway and consuming utility poles as if they were matchsticks. Finally, firefighters told the group they would have to get back in their cars and head for shelter in the Lake Tahoe area.

As Joe walked back to his car, a young man wearing a T-shirt and blue jeans approached him.

"Hey, you in the white shirt!" he called, referring to Joe.

Joe looked at him questioningly, pointing to himself and raising his eyebrows. "Me?"

The young man nodded and looked directly at Joe. "Yes. Don't worry. I got on your roof and watered it down for you."

Nearby, Tony flashed Joe a look of doubt. There had not been enough time for anyone to climb on either of their roofs. By the time they left, the flames had been crashing into their yards like a tidal wave. They had barely gotten away with their lives.

Joe shrugged in Tony's direction, convinced that the man must have confused him with someone else. Then he turned toward the young man once again. "Well, thanks. I sure appreciate that."

The man nodded, and walked toward the fire officials as Joe climbed into his car and drove away.

It took Joe more than an hour to wind his way down the mountain highway into Lake Tahoe and drive to a friend's house.

Then he collapsed into a chair and telephoned Janice's sister's house.

"Honey," he said, releasing a deep sigh. "I have some bad news."

He could think of nothing harder at that moment than telling his wife that her dream house had burned to the ground. But Janice handled it with the same show of faith that had helped him make it through the day.

"Thank God you're all right," was all she said.

The fire continued to burn through the night, making it impossible for Joe to return to Reno. Every hour or so he called the fire department seeking information about his house and asking whether it was safe to return, but no one knew the answers to his questions. Then, late that night, he remembered that the Fairchilds lived in the hills three miles across the valley from him. On a clear day they could see his house from their back window. He searched for their number and called them immediately.

At the Fairchilds' house, Betty and Chauncey continued to watch the fire through their binoculars long after they finished praying for Joe and his house. When the smoke cleared, what they saw amazed them. They wondered whether Joe was aware of what had happened.

When the telephone rang that evening, Chauncey answered it.

"Chauncey, it's Joe," he said, his tone urgent. "I was evacuated and had to drive to Lake Tahoe. Listen, can you see my house? How bad is it? Just tell me straight. I really need to know."

A grin broke out across Chauncey's face. "Joe, we watched the whole thing through our binoculars. We saw the flames change direction and head right for your house, so our whole family formed a prayer circle and prayed for your safety and the safety of your house." Chauncey paused a moment. "Joe, you won't believe this, but it's still standing. It looks absolutely untouched."

Joe immediately decided Chauncey was mistaking his house for another, and he was disappointed. He had hoped some part of the building might be saved, but he knew there was no way the entire house was still standing. The Fairchilds must have been watching someone else's home. It would have been miraculous if anything survived the firestorm that had descended on his property earlier that day.

Joe thought about the dry brush and wood that surrounded them there, and of the countless times Janice had asked him to clear the yard and cut back the brittle overgrowth. The truth was the Fairchilds probably couldn't see his house because there was simply nothing left to see.

"Well, thanks, Chauncey." Joe tried to sound optimistic. "I'll be back home as soon as they let me through, in case anyone asks about me."

The next morning, just after dawn, Joe learned it was finally safe to return. When he did, he was stunned by what he saw: The Fairchilds had been right.

The ferocious fire, flames towering higher than the treetops, had burned to within ten feet of his house and then abruptly stopped. All around his house the brush and wood that had cluttered his yard were destroyed, but the house and its contents were untouched. Joe felt almost as if he was seeing a vision of some kind and not the reality, even as he made his way around the house.

The power lines that fed electricity into the house were melted and telephone lines were fused together. But just a few feet closer to the house, the chicken coop was only scorched on the outside. Inside, all ten chickens were completely unharmed. And near the house Joe found his dog and two cats, scared but also not hurt by the fire. Even a little wooden bridge that led to Joe's house—surrounded by dry brush that had burned on both sides—remained standing without any sign of damage.

Then Joe spotted something else that was utterly incongruous considering what had happened the day before. The hose which he had dropped on his deck when he'd been forced to run for safety was now draped up over the house and lying on the roof.

In all, there were seven houses along the narrow hilly road

where Joe lived. Three were completely destroyed and three seriously damaged. Only Joe's house stood untouched, in the middle of a house-sized piece of the hillside that alone remained unburned.

In the weeks and months that followed, Joe spent a great deal of time wondering why his house had been spared. Research told him that the heat would have had to have been 1,800 degrees or hotter in order to melt the power lines. With temperatures that hot, the house should have burst into flames by spontaneous combustion from the heat alone. Yet not only was it unburned, it was also undamaged in every way.

The Fairchilds also were amazed when they got a closer view of Joe's house.

"To have seen Joe's house standing amidst all the blackened ruins that year was to know without a doubt that God had been there," Betty said later.

Indeed, Joe learned that three witnesses had seen someone on the roof after Joe and Tony fled the area. This made no logical sense: There was no ladder with which to climb on the roof, and no way water could have flowed from the Stevensons' well since power lines had been melted, thereby cutting off electricity to the electric water pump. Joe thought of the man who'd claimed to have watered down his roof, and wondered if God had heard the prayers around him and provided an angel who had supernaturally survived the fire and saved his house.

Whatever the truth was, the incident left Joe and the Fairchilds with several conclusions. First, even people who have faith sometimes don't have enough faith. In those instances, one's faith will sometimes be tested. And finally, when a person learns to thank God in the face of disaster and to place life unquestioningly in his hands, God can and will do astounding things in response to the simple but fervent prayers of everyday people.

ANSWER FIVE:

Alive for a Reason

*A*l Hammond was a high school sophomore in 1941 when his faith in God first became an all-consuming fire that burned deep inside him. Following the call, Al and his peers at University Christian Church in Los Angeles delved into community work. They helped children in the Watts section and other impoverished areas of the city, and told them the good news about God's love.

But for all the good Al and his friends in the high school youth group did over the next few years, by 1943 they had their eyes set on serving in another way. World War II was raging overseas, and they wanted to be a part of it. Before high school graduation, Al and several others from church enlisted in the Navy.

During the church group's last weekly meeting before the boys left for boot camp, their youth sponsor spoke about the duty they were about to perform for their country.

"To serve our country, fighting for freedom and

justice, is a calling of its own," she told the wide-eyed boys. Each one was nervous and excited about the journey they were about to take and the dangers that lay ahead.

"It will be easy to forget about God once you get involved in serving," she continued. "There will be temptations and times when no one around you is looking to God for help. But boys, whatever you do, don't forget God. He will be with you wherever you go.

"And remember that we who stay behind will be praying for you every day, for God's plan in your lives."

Several days later, after tearful good-byes, the boys from University Christian's youth group went their separate ways to different parts of the country where they would be trained and then sent into active duty.

Al was eighteen by then. He was sent to boot camp in Idaho, and from there to Norfolk, where he was placed with a division of enlistees who would be trained to specialize in submarine torpedoes. Although none of the boys from his church youth group were in the division, he did recognize one enlistee.

"Well, what do you know?" Al said when the two met up, exhausted after the first day of working at the torpedo station. It was Eddie, a boy who'd lived on the same street as Al when they were growing up. The two had been friends since junior high.

"Yeah." Eddie was still out of breath from just finishing an intense workout. He leaned his head over the drinking fountain and sucked in as much water as he could. "Looks like we'll be submarine men together, huh?"

The presence of each other made Al and Eddie feel less homesick, even though after the first few weeks they had made dozens of friends in the unit. Rather than just a random group of enlisted men, the division quickly developed a sense of unity which would inevitably help them as they worked toward the day when they would be assigned to the same submarine.

For three months the men worked together; all that time, Al never forgot the words of his church's youth minister. Indeed there were temptations, but when the guys in his division would set out for a night on the town, he stayed back at the barracks.

"Nothing good waitin' for me out there," he'd tell Eddie and the others when they badgered him to join in the trips to town.

"All right," they'd say, respecting him too much to give him a hard time. "But you'll be sorry when you hear what you missed."

Al was never sorry. He intended to stay true to his moral convictions. Still, something *had* changed about the intensity of his faith. He no longer talked about God, and as boot camp continued, his beliefs became locked inside a private part of him that no one else knew existed. Sometimes he thought of his church friends, and he knew that somewhere in Los Angeles they were still praying for him, for God's plan in his life. But each day he fell into bed exhausted, with little time to pray and no time at all for studying scripture.

Three months passed, and Al's division was sent to Norfolk, Virginia, to the Navy's high-tech torpedo training school. There, as Al spent still less time thinking about his faith in God, the young men immersed themselves in a crash course in submarine torpedoes.

Three weeks before they were shipped out, the Navy conducted a specialized physical exam to be sure the enlisted men's ears could take the pressure of living and working deep beneath the surface of the ocean. One at a time the men subjected themselves to the pressure test, and each passed easily. Then it was Al's turn.

"Okay, son, you'll feel some pressure in your ears as we do this test," barked the instructor who was administering it. "Then you'll need to perform certain tasks related to the operation of a submarine. Shouldn't be any problems."

But as the test began, Al was struck with excruciating pain in one ear. He tried at first to work through the burning in his head, but as the minutes passed blood began trickling from his ear down the side of his face.

"That's enough," the instructor said when the test was finished. Then he turned to Al. "Son, you got something wrong with that ear?"

Al thought a moment, and then remembered. When he had been a young child a firecracker had exploded very near his ear. Whenever he had a head cold or was subject to pressure for any reason, his ear became excruciatingly painful. But until now, he had never considered how the pressure of being underwater might affect it.

Al explained his history to the instructor, and waited anxiously for a response.

"Well, I hate to do this son, believe me," the man said as he scratched Al's name off the list of men taking the test. "But you just failed the physical because of that ear of yours. You couldn't spend ten minutes underwater with an ear like that."

Al was crushed. He had become very close with the men in the submarine division, and was only weeks away from being assigned to active duty. Instead, he bade the others good-bye and wished them luck.

"You keep the guys in line," he told Eddie the day he left. "And after we win this thing I'll see you back home."

Because of his special training in torpedoes, Al was eventually assigned to work on the S.S. *Barnegat*, a specialized ship designated for the conduction of torpedo tests. At that time, the torpedoes used by the United States were designed so that if they missed a target they would continue dangerously into the ocean, sometimes hitting American vessels. The crew aboard the *Barnegat* was chosen to test and perfect an exploding device that would enable torpedoes to be drawn into the magnetic field of enemy ships, destroying them even if the original shot was not on target.

Instead of serving in the war zone, the *Barnegat* sailed the calm, relatively friendly waters of Coco Solo, Panama, firing torpedoes filled not with explosives, but with water. Divers would then retrieve the torpedoes so that naval engineers could study the results of the test. A slight change would be made in the exploding device, and then Al and the others would prepare for another test.

Al knew it was important work, and there were certainly times when it was interesting. But still, he was bitterly disappointed about missing his opportunity to be on a submarine in the Atlantic or Pacific where the war was being fought. He thought often of his friends from that division, and wondered how they were faring against the enemy.

Occasionally he still thought of his friends back at University Christian Church. And true to his beliefs, he remained morally strong. But months had passed since he'd attended a church service.

One afternoon Al was standing too near a large gun when it suddenly went off. The explosion ripped into his eardrum like a knife. Again blood dripped from the injured ear, and Al was ordered to report to sick bay. While he was being attended to, he overheard one of the petty officers talking with several of the sick men about God. Suddenly Al remembered hearing about this man. Everyone called him Arkie because he was from Arkansas, and each week he conducted a simple church service and held Bible studies in the sick bay.

Arkie's voice was intense, and there was a light in his eyes that held Al mesmerized. Suddenly, he was overwhelmed with remorse. His eyes had once glowed just as brightly; his desire to share God's love had once been just as sincere. But since enlisting he had let the light grow dim and the sincerity silent. His church friends were still praying for him; he was sure of it. And he wondered if hearing Arkie might have been God's way of answering those prayers. Maybe the time had come for his now-cold faith to be renewed.

Al pondered this for several days until arrangements could be made to fly him back to Florida for further medical attention. Not long after arriving in the States, Al sought out the wall where updates on the war were posted. Feeling very removed from the action, Al anxiously looked forward to reading the reports.

He scanned the first few items, and then his eyes grew wide and he felt his heart beating wildly in his chest. The submarine with his former division aboard was listed as missing in action.

His face ashen, Al turned and found a place to sit down. When the enemy sunk a submarine, there was no fiery ship sinking slowly into the ocean. The deed was done underwater, and often left little in the way of identifiable remains. For that reason, if a submarine was listed as missing in action, it usually meant one thing. The vessel had been destroyed in unknown waters, in this case somewhere in the Pacific.

Tears filled his eyes as he thought of the men he'd trained with and teased with, eaten and lived with as though they were one large family. Of all of them, only he had been spared.

"Dear God," he whispered in despair. "Why me? Why did they all have to die and yet I am still alive? Why, Lord?"

In that instant everything that had happened in the past months came together. He thought about the men in his division and his own reluctance to share his faith with any of them. Then he thought of Arkie and the light in his eyes. And finally of the submarine with all his friends aboard, all of them killed in the line of duty.

Eventually the memory of his lost friends helped Al understand what God wanted him to do with his life. He would finish serving in the Navy, and when the war ended he would return to Los Angeles and enroll in Bible college. Then he would spend his life working as a missionary, allowing the fire that had once burned so brightly inside him to gather strength and remain unextinguished for a lifetime.

Al believed beyond a doubt that the reason he had been spared was because God had heard his church colleagues' prayers. His former youth sponsor had been right. God had a plan for his life.

Six years passed. Al was discharged from the Navy in December 1945, having served until the very end of the war. After that he followed his convictions, earning a degree at San Jose Bible College, where he met and became engaged to a woman named Eleanor Reineke. The couple both felt that God had called them to be missionaries, but they had no idea where they would serve.

Then in December 1951, Al again experienced strong evidence of God's hand on his life.

He and Eleanor were driving through the Santa Cruz Mountains toward a small Christian camp. The roads were narrow and damp from a week of recent rain, and the couple prayed aloud for safety. Just before they reached the camp they turned onto a remote section of roadway, and drove for miles before realizing they were lost. Just when they were about to turn back, a section of the road collapsed and the couple's Chevy sedan tumbled down 150 feet into the canyon below.

Battered and bloodied, Al and Eleanor scrambled from the wreckage and made their way through the mud back to the top of the hill. Al could see that Eleanor was in great pain, and he knew there was no way she could walk back to the main road. *Oh, dear God,* he prayed silently, *help us get out of here and get Eleanor to a hospital. Please, God.*

Almost at once a car appeared around the bend, stopping just before the area where the road had given way. A man inside climbed out and lowered his jacket to Al.

"Here," he shouted. "Grab this. I'll help you up."

Using the jacket as a rope, Al helped Eleanor up the hill. Drawing from his last bit of strength, he then pulled himself up.

Eleanor lay across the man's backseat unconscious, and Al joined her, dazed by the accident. But for all the pain and confusion, he was keenly aware of one thing. God had answered his prayers and provided help almost immediately.

In less than an hour the couple arrived at the hospital emergency room in Santa Cruz, and Al learned that Eleanor had suffered a broken back but was not paralyzed in any way. Al's injuries were also serious, and he had lost a great deal of blood, but he was released later that day, expected to make a full recovery.

"What about the man who brought us here?" Al asked the emergency room nurse. "If he hadn't stopped and picked us up, we never would have made it."

"He came in and told us he needed help," the nurse said. Her face was puzzled as she continued. "Several of us followed him to his car and helped get you and your friend out of his backseat. When we went back out to get his name he was gone. Didn't leave any information whatsoever."

Later, when Eleanor had recovered enough to talk about the accident, she told Al she was certain God had sent an angel to help them that afternoon. Al considered the possibility, and realized how quickly God had helped them heal from their physical injuries.

"You know, El," he told her one day, shortly after they were married that spring. "Sometimes in life there are more than just physical wounds that need healing. I still miss my friends who were killed in the war, I still think about them. But I also think about the people who were our enemies. Like the Japanese. They were responsible for the deaths of my friends, but they're hurting just like we are. Maybe it's time to heal."

Again Al remembered the way his church friends had prayed for him so long ago. The words of his former youth minister echoed in Al's head.

"Remember that we who stay behind will be praying for you every day, for God's plan in your lives."

Suddenly the destination of his mission was clear. For the next two years he and Eleanor made plans and financial preparations. Then in the spring of 1954, ten years after losing his friends in the war with Japan, Al Hammond and his family set off for fourteen years of missionary work in the one country where he felt God wanted him most. It was a country where Al knew the people were hungry for God's message of hope. A place where love and forgiveness and healing were in short supply—especially from Americans.

That country was Japan.

ANSWER SIX:

Going Home

*J*oy Gladish was the only one of her five siblings who never quite fit in. When her four sisters played sports with their only brother, she watched on the sidelines; when the girls grew older and began dating, Joy stayed at home and watched television. She felt too shy and unlovely to mix with boys her age.

She struggled with her weight, and often sat alone at family get-togethers, feeling too self-conscious to participate. And so her peers and even her immediate family often forgot about her, finding it easier to be involved in their own lives than to take time to figure out why Joy was so quiet.

During those crucial formative years, Joy appeared to have few opinions and even fewer social graces, but inside her lived a young woman nearly bursting with the desire to be loved and cared for. For that reason, from the time she was old enough to walk, she idolized the two men in her life: her brother, Stephen, and her father, Don.

Don Gladish was a small-town doctor during the years when his family was growing up in Glenview, Illinois. He was the type of practitioner who still made house calls and who allowed his patients to pay him by whatever means they could—even if that meant trading a handpicked bag of produce for one of his visits. He had the lowest charges in town, and while most doctors would only prescribe medications, he was willing to teach people nutrition and preventive measures to improve their health.

Everyone in town loved Doctor Don, as they called him. The feeling was mutual, and he often spent seven days a week engulfed in his practice. Just a handful of people in Glenview ever wondered if Doctor Don loved them in return and most of them lived under his roof.

"Don't you ever wonder, Stephen?" Joy asked her brother one day when they were in their early teens. "He's gone so much of the time that I'm not sure whether he really loves us or not."

Stephen's eyes fell, and he stared at the baseball and glove in his hands. His father had promised to play ball with him that day, but once again he'd been called away for a medical emergency.

"Yeah," he said after a while. "I know what you mean. If he loves us, then why can't he spend more time with us? It seems like he should want to be with us more than with his patients."

Don was such a happy, good-natured man that the children felt foolish voicing any complaints at all except to each other. But they still missed their father, and wondered about how much he loved them.

Years passed, and Don's health fizzled rapidly. He had been diagnosed in the late 1950s with a disease that made him prone to seizures. But it wasn't until ten years later that he began degenerating and finally had to give up his practice.

He died in 1967; throughout the final days of his life it was often Joy and Stephen who took turns waiting on him and comforting him.

"What are we going to do without him?" Joy asked her brother one afternoon. "I can't imagine living without him around."

Stephen nodded. Their family had been raised to love God and obey the Bible. He knew that his father would be in Heaven when he died, but still, the pain of losing him was almost too much to bear.

"I don't know, Joy," he said, putting an arm around her heavyset shoulders. "But I know that what Dad taught us is true. He'll be in Heaven and one day we'll go to live with him there, and we'll all be together again."

Joy smiled through her tears. "Yeah, and in Heaven he won't have to make house calls."

In the decade that followed, Joy's sisters each went their own way while Joy became very attached to her brother. Shortly after Stephen joined the Air Force, she, too, joined. When they had both served their time, Stephen married, taught college, and eight years later moved to Tucson, where he began working on his second master's degree, at the University of Arizona.

After serving a double hitch in the Air Force, Joy moved to Tucson and found a house just a few miles from Stephen's. Not long afterward she, too, began attending the university.

"I know she wants to get married and have a family of her own," Stephen confided to his wife, Betsy, one day. "But all she does is go to school, work, and sit home in front of the television set. She can't expect to meet someone living like that."

Betsy angled her head thoughtfully. "You know, Stephen, I think it's just going to take more time with Joy. She's starting to come out of her shell some, and once she has her degree she'll feel a lot better about things. Don't worry about her."

Besides, it wasn't as if Joy didn't have a family. She did. Over the next fifteen years Stephen and Betsy raised four children, and Joy was always at the center of their family outings.

Over time, Joy earned a bachelor's degree in rehabilitation and began working in an alcohol-recovery center. Her patients ranged from hopeless adults to troubled teens, and Joy worked tirelessly with them. Sometimes, when a patient would ask her personal questions, she would share her faith.

"God is the only one who really knows us and loves us unconditionally," she would tell those patients. "For most of us, our lives start getting back on track the day we start loving him in return."

As Joy became more involved with her patients, Stephen and Betsy began to notice a change in her.

"You know," Stephen said one night as he and his wife were washing dinner dishes together at the kitchen sink, "all of us kids growing up used to think there was something wrong with Joy. We thought she'd never amount to much. I guess because she was so alone and never did the things the rest of us did."

He paused a moment before continuing. "But that isn't true at all. She's got her education and a wonderful job. She gives hope to people who have none, and for dozens of her patients she's the greatest gift God has ever given them."

"I told you, Stephen," Betsy said warmly. "You used to worry so much about Joy."

"I still worry about her because she has no family of her own. All she's ever really wanted is a family."

"She's growing at her own pace." Betsy smiled, drying her hands on a nearby towel and setting it back on the countertop. "For now, though, it's not like she has no one. We're her family. But one of these days, when she's ready, she will meet the right person and then she'll have her family. She has plenty of time yet. Watch and see."

But a few years later, in 1988, Joy was diagnosed with breast cancer. At forty-three, she was younger than most breast cancer patients, so doctors were at first hopeful that she might survive. They removed a cancerous section of her breast, and when the cancer continued to spread they performed a mastectomy. The surgery was followed up by chemotherapy and radiation treatments, which caused Joy's hair to fall out and often left her violently ill.

Still, she continued to work, staying home only on the days when she felt sickest. When she was at work, she put her personal troubles behind her and concentrated only on helping her patients.

"That woman is amazing," Betsy said one day in early 1992 as she watched Joy making dinner for her family in the kitchen.

Stephen stared thoughtfully at his sister. "She's a fighter, all right. But I'm so worried about her, Betsy."

"The cancer?"

Stephen nodded. "She talked to the doctor yesterday. It's spread into her lymph system."

Betsy hung her head and sighed, and for a long time neither of them said anything. There was no need. They both knew what the news meant. When cancer spread through the lymph system as it had in Joy's body, the outcome was too often certain.

Joy continued to work through the first part of March, before succumbing to her illness and taking a leave of absence. The cancer had continued to spread, this time beyond her lymph system into her entire body, and doctors did not expect her to live more than six months.

Now, when Stephen visited Joy at her apartment, their time together was painful for both of them.

"Joy, you've got to hang in there and pull through this," Stephen would tell her as he sat at the edge of her bed and helped her take sips of ice water. She had lost a lot of weight and her skin looked gray and lifeless.

"I'm trying, Stephen, really I am," she would say, never complaining about the effort it took to muster her strength.

When Stephen would leave Joy's apartment, he would often bow his head and pray before driving home.

"Lord, please help me see Joy through this terrible disease. I pray that she lives. But if her time has come to go home to you, I pray you make the transition easy. Please don't let her suffer, Lord."

Throughout April and much of May, Stephen would get off work early and stop to visit Joy. Although her body was obviously deteriorating, she was not bedridden, and Stephen was thankful for that. After their visit he would normally return home for dinner and then go back to see Joy later in the evening, sometimes bringing her a plate of whatever they'd eaten that night.

"It's getting to me, Betsy," he confided to his wife one morning. "I hate to see her falling apart. One of these days she's going to be too weak to get off the couch, and then what are we going to do?"

Betsy thought a moment. "Well, we could have her come live with us."

Stephen had thought of the possibility, but knew it would be difficult to make it work. Each of their three bedrooms was being used, and there wouldn't be anyone home during the day to take care of Joy. Still, he wanted her to feel welcome. If there was any way they could figure out the logistics, having Joy come live with them was really the only option Stephen could imagine.

That week he told Joy about the idea.

"No way, Stephen, not on your life," she said, trying to sound firm. "You and Betsy and the kids have been my family for such a long time; you've done so much for me," she continued, struggling with each word because of her weakened condition. "I'm not going to impose on you now and make you change your whole house around just so I can come there to die."

"Joy, don't talk like that," Stephen chided her gently. "You're going to pull through this. You've had hard times before, but you've always fought it."

But both brother and sister knew there was no truth in his words. That much was clear as the end of May drew near and Joy finally became unable to leave her bed except for a brief period once or twice each day.

"Listen, Joy, if you won't come and live with me and Betsy, then you need to move to the Veterans' Hospice or someplace where you can have help around the clock," Stephen said when he visited her. "It's eating me up knowing you're here alone and going through so much pain by yourself."

"Stephen, I'm fine," Joy insisted. "I can reach my medication and I have water by me all the time. I get Meals on Wheels and whatever you bring me. That's plenty of food. I don't need any help."

Stephen disagreed, and his sister's situation weighed heavily on him. He prayed often about a solution for Joy's living arrangements, asking God to show him what to do for her.

"God, you know her heart, and I pray you convince her to give up her independence. She needs help, Lord, and I can't provide it all. I don't want her living alone, so please help us to work things out. Help her to be willing to move if that's what is necessary. Amen."

Finally, one afternoon later that week, Stephen left a message for Joy's doctor, Dr. Marilyn Croghan, to call him. He planned to ask the doctor to have a talk with Joy. Maybe she could convince Joy that she needed to leave her apartment and get help.

The next morning, Dr. Croghan returned Stephen's call.

"Yes, this is Joy's brother, Stephen," he said.

"Hello, Stephen. We're all very fond of Joy," she said politely. "How can I help you?"

"First of all, I think she's getting worse very quickly and I'm concerned about her," he said.

"She's lost some mobility," Dr. Croghan explained. "But I still think she's got another three months or more."

"That's why I'm calling. See, I've asked her to come live with me and my family, but she won't do it. She thinks she'll be in the way, and I haven't been able to change her mind." Stephen drew in a deep breath. "I called because I was hoping you might be able to talk some sense into her. If she won't come live with me, she needs to be at a hospice or a group home, someplace where she can have help around the clock."

Dr. Croghan thought for a moment before responding. "Have you considered helping her move in with your father?" she asked.

Stephen's face twisted in confusion, and he was not sure he had heard the doctor correctly. "What?"

"Maybe it's time she go and live with your father," the doctor repeated. "Sometime around February, I got a call from a man who said he was Joy's father. He wanted to know how she was doing, and he seemed very knowledgeable about her particular case. We chatted for a few minutes. Before we finished talking, he told me that when things got really bad people shouldn't worry about Joy because she would be going home to live with him."

Stephen had no idea what to say. He said nothing.

"Mr. Gladish? Are you there?"

Stephen cleared his throat. "Dr. Croghan, my father died in 1967. There's no way he could have made that phone call."

"How strange," she said. "Wait. Just a minute." There was a rustling sound of paper as Dr. Croghan located Joy's file.

"Okay, here it is. Let me see. Yes, it's right here. On February 12th I received a call on my cellular car phone from a Dr. Don Gladish. The man said he was Joy's father and that when she got toward the end of her illness she'd be going home to live with him."

Stephen shook his head, trying to make sense of the situation. "That's fine, Dr. Croghan, but my father's been dead for twenty-five years. Obviously he couldn't make a phone call."

"Is it possible it was an uncle or some other relative or friend?" she asked. "As I said, the man was very knowledgeable about Joy and her condition. I never mentioned the call to Joy because I assumed your father had discussed it with her before calling me."

There was silence between them again. "Doctor, you're sure the man said he was Joy's father?"

"Definitely. I remember the call very clearly. I'm sure it must have been an uncle or something. Either way, why don't you look into it and let me know. It sounds like somewhere there's a family member who is expecting her to come home to live with them.

Meanwhile I'll work on Joy and try to convince her that it isn't wise for her to be alone anymore."

Stephen hung up the phone and sat staring at it, wondering who would have made such a call. There were several uncles in the Gladish family, but none of them knew Joy very well, and certainly none of them would have identified themselves as Joy's father. Nevertheless, he spent much of the day contacting every male relative who knew Joy and asking if anyone had made the call. By that evening he had learned that none of them knew anything about it.

Suddenly he remembered his prayer. He had asked God to work out Joy's living arrangements, and now he had discovered that Dr. Croghan had received a phone call from someone claiming to be Don Gladish. Was it possible that God had answered his prayers by letting him know that Joy was eventually going to be going home to Heaven, where she would be reunited with their father?

Stephen told Betsy what had happened, and she, too, thought it might be possible. Perhaps, she said, the phone call was God's way of letting them know Joy was headed for a better place.

"But that doesn't help us right now," she added. "We still don't know where she needs to be for the next three months until she dies. She needs a place to live, Stephen."

"I know. That's the strange part. If it's an answer to prayer, then what do we do about the next three months?"

The answer came too quickly.

Early on Memorial Day, Joy died peacefully in her sleep. She had finally been completely bedridden for just two days.

Dr. Croghan and the others were baffled when they heard the news. Although she had been very clearly dying, they thought Joy should have had at least another three months to live.

At the Gladish home, the news of Joy's death sent Stephen and Betsy on a roller-coaster ride of mixed emotions.

"I miss her so much," Stephen said, his eyes brimming with

tears. "But she was no longer able to live alone, and God knew it was time for her to come home."

"It makes you wonder, doesn't it?" Betsy asked.

Stephen raised an eye. "About the phone call, you mean? Yeah, it does. The more I think about it, the more I believe it just might have been Dad making that phone call."

"Maybe so."

"Really," Stephen continued. "I believe God wanted us to know everything was going to work out fine. Joy wouldn't need a place to live because she was going home to Heaven."

Betsy was silent, lost in her own thoughts.

"You know something, Betsy?" Stephen said. "I always wondered if Dad really loved me. Joy wondered the same thing. But now I feel like I can put that behind me. God knew that I wondered about my Dad and his true feelings for me. So he answered my prayer and let me know that Dad did love both of us. He loved us so much that he was looking forward to welcoming the first of his children home."

Divinely Directed

Steve Moss was a purist when it came to backpacking. He would set a weight limit for his pack and weigh each item before placing it inside. If something was too heavy, another thing had to be left behind.

"Only take what is absolutely necessary," he would tell his wife, Toni, when they planned a backpacking trip together.

She would nod, partially dreading the mountain trails and the effort it took to hike with a pack strapped to her back.

Still, for twenty years she accompanied him, stifling her complaints and bearing up under the strain of the sport. She loved the outdoors as much as her husband, and would not have wanted to miss the trips. She only wished there were an easier way to travel.

Then, soon after their children left home, Toni discovered the perfect solution.

"I'll take my horse," she said, grinning broadly.

"What? How're we going to backpack with you on a horse?" Steve wrinkled his nose curiously.

"I'll carry the gear on a saddlebag and ride the horse while you walk along beside me."

Steve raised an eyebrow warily. "That's not much fun for you," he said.

"Oh, you have no idea how much fun that'd be for me. I could savor the smell of the pines and enjoy every bit of the beauty around me. No more sweating, no more steep mountain grades where my legs feel like rubber bands. It'll be perfect."

Toni had ridden horses since she was a young girl. But until then she had never considered taking her horse on a backpacking trip. After their first trip with Toni's horse she knew she'd never backpack on foot again.

For the next few years, whenever Steve and Toni went backpacking, Toni rode her horse and Steve hiked alongside her. But during that time Steve's health began to deteriorate. He had been diagnosed with multiple sclerosis several years earlier, and in recent months he'd grown unable to walk distances that had once been easy for him.

"Steve, why don't you get a horse so you can backpack my way?" Toni suggested one afternoon when they were taking yet another break so Steve could rest.

"That's not backpacking, Toni, and you know it," he returned. "I'd rather do it the right way, even if I have to go a little slower."

But eventually, Steve's purist attitude toward backpacking eroded. He was not ready to give up his sojourns into nature, even if his body was no longer capable of carrying him.

So in 1992, he and Toni bought another horse, a calm animal whom Steve named Traveler. Over the next two years Steve learned to ride, and finally on Memorial Day weekend 1994, they set out for a three-day backpacking trip via horseback in the Sierra Nevada Mountains.

The plan was for Steve and Toni to start from Kennedy Meadows—located in the High Sierra range—and ride five miles up into Clover Meadow, which is only accessible by foot or on horseback.

The trip up was uneventful, and Toni was thankful as always that the horses had climbed the rocky switchback trails with relative ease. They reached Clover Meadow that evening and set up camp.

"How're you feeling?" Toni asked her husband, aware that even riding horseback might be enough to tire him because of his illness.

"Fine." He smiled as he removed Traveler's saddle. "I don't know why I fought you on this for so long. It's great taking the trails by horseback."

That evening the couple ate dinner adjacent to a lush meadow, and Toni untied the horses so they could graze in a leisurely manner. After an hour, she tied them back up and she and Steve turned in for the night.

Early the next morning Toni crawled out of the tent and found the horses restless, apparently still hungry from the previous day's climb.

"Okay, boys," she said softly, patting the horses gently. She untied them from the fence post. "Go eat."

For the next ten minutes the horses ate contentedly. Then, for no apparent reason, one of them began running in the opposite direction across the meadow. The second horse followed, and within minutes the pair had disappeared from sight.

Panic coursed through Toni's body. They were miles from their car, with a hundred pounds of camping gear and horse equipment. Without the horses there was no way they could make it back down the trail—especially with Steve's condition. Toni ran back to camp and grabbed two lead ropes and a bag of grain.

"The horses are gone," she shouted to Steve, who was just emerging from the tent. "I'm going to go find them."

Then she took off, running across the meadow to the place where she had last seen the horses. Her heart pounded in her chest, and she felt like she was suffocating from the panic that gripped her. The farther she ran, the more meadow she could see, but the horses were nowhere to be found.

Toni knew that if she didn't force herself to calm down, she would be useless at solving their dilemma. As her panic threatened to overtake her, she willed herself to turn to God.

"Lord, please help me find the horses," she muttered, out of breath. Toni had been a believer for many years, but never had she felt such desperation for God's immediate help. "Please give me a clue, show me where they are."

She stopped running, and her eyes caught something on the ground. A hoofprint. Her heart soared with thanks and she began to follow a barely visible trail of prints. After ten minutes she reached the boggy edge of Clover Meadow. There the trail fizzled.

"Okay, Lord, what should I do now?" she said aloud, exhausted and still fighting the fear that threatened to engulf her. She climbed up a rocky outcropping for a better view, and realized too late that the way up was steep and tiring. Throughout the climb she was continually tempted to think of the negative possibilities of the situation rather than her faith.

Finally she reached the top and saw another widespread valley below, far larger than the meadow she had just crossed. She analyzed the situation, and realized that if the horses had crossed that valley they would have had to go from south to north. She was on the east end, and figured if she set out across it and found even one hoofprint, she would have a trail to follow.

"Lord, please show me a clear hoofprint so I will know that I'm in the right place," she begged, tears of frustration filling her eyes. "The horses could be anywhere."

Painstakingly, she climbed down the rocks into the valley and began walking. She had nearly reached the halfway point when she spotted a single hoofprint among the rocks and sparse grass in the meadow. The horses had indeed come that way, and she felt suddenly calmer. The animals could have gone in any direction, but God was leading her in the right one.

Toni followed the hoofprints for a while, but then she became very tired. She slowed her pace and finally stopped, listening to the wind echo across the desolate meadow and straining to hear the horses.

"Please God, let me hear them," she whispered. "Let me know if they're miles away or somewhere nearby."

She waited, and in less than a minute the horses came galloping up over a hill. Stunned, she held up the bag of grain and the pair cantered directly to her. She opened the bag and let them eat as she snapped the leads around their necks. Relief flooded her body, and she gazed open-faced, toward heaven.

"Thank you," she whispered, the words taking on a fresh meaning. "Thank you for hearing me, Lord."

During her long walk back to camp with the horses she had time to reflect on what had happened. Each time she had prayed for help, a hoofprint had been revealed inches away. And when her faith had all but vanished, the horses themselves had appeared.

"I learned something out there," she told Steve after she returned to camp. "God is in control of things. We're not. I was so tempted to panic, and if I'd done that we wouldn't have our horses right now. But if we trust God and ask for his help, he hears us. He really hears us."

A Prayer in the Cornfield

*T*hat summer the drought was the worst one anyone in the Geisbert family could remember. For more than two hundred years the Geisberts had been farming land in central Maryland, and Roger Geisbert had followed the family tradition. He was seventy-six that summer of 1964, and he and his wife survived off the crops produced by a small twenty-two-acre farm. But with no rain for weeks on end and high temperatures breaking records, his crops were disintegrating before his eyes.

First the hay had gone, and next the barley. Then his wheat crop had succumbed to the drought. Now Roger had just one crop left: the corn. Every day Roger would walk to the farthest corner of his farm where the corn stood in long even rows. There he would assess the damage caused by the lack of rain. Although the stalks looked tall and healthy, the cobs had just begun to develop when the drought set in. Now the stalks were dry and brittle, and the bases of the cobs were beginning to wither. According to Roger's analysis, the corn could only survive a few more days before the crop would be a complete waste.

One morning that week Roger climbed out of bed, slipped into his overalls, and checked the sky outside. Only a few solitary white clouds marred an otherwise completely blue horizon.

"Ma," he muttered softly, glancing toward his wife. "I'm gonna go check the corn."

Roger ambled out the front door, still as able-bodied as he had been twenty years earlier. He wound his way through rows of dead crops until he reached the corn. Carefully he rubbed his fingers on either side of one of the stocks. The leaves were pale green and stiff from the lack of water. Next he gently peeled back the husks until he could see the corn developing on the cob beneath. The kernels were small and puckered, with space between them.

Painstakingly Roger made his way through the cornfield, sampling various stalks and checking for drought damage. As he did he remembered what his father had said about the importance of the corn crop.

"A farmer can lose just about every other crop he has and still survive," his father would say. "As long as he keeps his corn."

Roger had learned the wisdom of that lesson time and again over the years. Corn was almost a double crop for small farmers like himself. First the cobs could be harvested and sold, eaten, used in baking, and used to feed certain farm animals. Then the stalks could be harvested and used to feed other farm animals.

His father had also said that corn was a good crop because it didn't need a lot of rain to do well.

"Thing is," he could hear his father saying, "it needs rain at the right time."

Roger had also seen that truth play out over the years. He knew from experience that his corn needed rain that very day if the cobs were to have a chance.

Discouraged by the uniform dryness throughout his cornfield, Roger finally hung his head and turned back toward the farmhouse. He could see the ruin and pain that lay ahead of them when the crops failed. He took several steps and then—beside himself with despair—he fell to one knee. Leaning forward, he dug his elbows into the once-rich soil and with drying stalks of corn all around him, he began to pray.

"Lord, you know me now even as you have known me since birth. You know my shortcomings and you know my weaknesses. And certainly you know my desperate need for rain. Lord, the crop will fail; we could lose the farm. We need rain, dear Lord, and we need it today."

Roger waited a moment before standing. A single tear formed in his eye and rolled down one weather-beaten cheek, slipping and sliding across the crevices in his worn face. All his life he had been a praying man, but on this day he needed God's reassurance more than any time in his life.

"One more thing, Lord," he continued. "If you've heard me today, please show me."

Then, moving even more slowly than before, Roger struggled to his feet and trudged toward the farmhouse.

Suddenly, with just a few hundred yards between him and the front door, there was a sharp flash of lightning and a loud crackling of thunder. Roger jumped back, unsure of what he had seen. The lightning looked to have been very close, possibly somewhere between him and the house.

"Must have been heat lightning," Roger said out loud. He looked warily toward the sky, but the only cloud in the area was an almost transparent white cumulus cotton ball off to the left. Certain that there was no danger of another bolt of lightning, Roger set off again toward the house.

The moment he set foot on the porch, rain began to fall. Roger's mouth hung open in shock as he looked upward once more at the blue sky. He stuck his arm out and felt the water penetrating his sleeve. For several minutes the rain fell, and then just as quickly as it had started it stopped again.

Roger rushed into the house. "Ma," he shouted, moving excitedly into the kitchen where his wife was preparing breakfast. "Ma, you won't believe this. I was out there looking at our corn, knowing it wasn't going to last but another day if we didn't get some rain down here pretty quick.

"Well, about that time I dropped to my knees and prayed, asked the dear Lord to send us some rain. I even asked him to let me know that he'd heard my prayer."

His wife raised a skeptical eye. "You don't mean to tell me it just rained outside? From a clear blue sky?"

"That's exactly what I mean to tell you." He pointed to the wet droplet markings on his denim shirt sleeve. "If I hadn't been standing on the porch my whole shirt'd been soaked."

Then, without waiting for a response from his wife, Roger headed directly to his bedroom and fell on his knees. This time his prayer was one of thanks.

"Lord, I know that rain just now came directly from you and that you did indeed hear my prayer," Roger said, his voice quiet and filled with awe. "But Lord, as you know, we'll need even more to keep us going. Please, Lord. Send us more rain."

The forecast that night called for several days of nothing but sunshine, but the next morning Roger awoke to the sound of steady rain. He stepped out of bed and moved toward the window, where he saw rain clouds gathered across the sky.

"Ma, you know our God is so good that he didn't just send any old kind of rain," Roger said, brimming with excitement. "He sent us a good old-fashioned soaking rain. Not a pelting rain where you get all kinds of runoff. But the kind that seeps way down deep to the roots of the crop. Our corn's gonna be just fine."

The rain continued at that steady pace all day and into the night. Four times during the day Roger stopped and walked outside to the covered porch, gazing across his corn crop, and marveled at the rain that soaked his fields. Each time, when he returned back inside the house, he went straight to his bedroom and knelt by his bed.

"Lord, I don't know what I ever did to deserve this, but I want to thank you right proper," he'd say, his head bowed, his voice humble. "I know without a doubt that this rain comes as an answer to my prayer and, well, I thank you with all my being."

Before the week was finished Roger had checked enough of his corn to know that the rain had done its job. No longer did the stalks feel dry. Instead they were thick and flexible, filled with the precious moisture. He peeled back the husks just far enough to get a glimpse of the corn, and saw plump, moist kernels filling the cob.

"One more week, Ma, and that corn'll be ready to pick," Roger told his wife that afternoon. "Nothing like a miracle crop to finish the season."

A week later Roger began the tedious process of tying stalks into bundles, tearing the cobs free, and placing them in piles throughout the field. Next he worked himself from one pile of corn to another, husking the ears and placing them into a wagon.

The husking process was almost mechanical for Roger, who had worked around corn much of his life. It took him just seconds to tear off the husks. As he threw one cob into the corn pile on the wagon, he was already reaching for another ear.

That day he started early in the morning at the farthest corner of his farm and worked his way toward the house—it was habitual with him, and he'd done that the day he'd knelt down and prayed for rain in the cornfield. Just before noon he was working on a pile of corn when he felt one of the husked ears shake as he tossed it on the pile.

Puzzled, Roger stopped his work, stood up, and walked around to where the ear of corn had fallen.

"Must have been a mouse or some other kind of varmint," he mumbled to himself.

But as Roger gazed down at the corn he saw something entirely unexpected. The cob he had just finished husking was made up of brilliant yellow kernels with the exception of a handful of kernels that were red. Occasionally his corn crop would contain a few ears of red corn, and once in a while a cob might have a mix of yellow and red kernels. But this one was different.

The red kernels were set in two neat rows forming the most perfect cross Roger had ever seen.

Slowly he stood up, holding the corn gingerly in his hand. As he got his bearings he realized that he was in almost exactly the same spot where he'd knelt and prayed that afternoon two weeks earlier.

Roger carried the corn into the house and showed it in awe to his wife.

"I asked God to let me know that he had heard me that afternoon," Roger said, his eyes brimming with tears. "And I thought he did that by sending the rain. Now I get this."

Roger walked across the room to the telephone and called his nephew Paul Geisbert, Sr. Paul was a dairy farmer with a larger farm not quite four miles from where Roger lived. The two men had always been close because of their shared interest in carrying on the Geisbert farming tradition, and because Paul often lent Roger a hand on his farm. In fact, Paul had helped plant the corn, and before the season was over he would help his uncle with the harvest.

"Paul?" Roger said, his voice cracking.

"Yes, sir?" Paul answered. He was fifty-six that year and had grown children of his own. But he held a deep respect for his Uncle Roger, and it showed in their conversation.

"Paul, you must come right away," Roger continued. "I'll be waiting outside."

Paul hung up the phone and stared speechless at his wife, Fern.

"I wonder what's wrong with Uncle Roger," he finally said, his face concerned. "He sounds like he's crying."

Paul climbed into his pickup truck, and in under ten minutes he pulled up outside his uncle's farmhouse. Roger stood outside near the garage. As Paul approached, he could see that his uncle was holding an ear of corn. He could also see that the man's hands were shaking.

Roger explained to his nephew how he had prayed for rain

and received it immediately, and how he had asked God to let him know that his prayers had been heard.

Paul examined the perfect cross made of red kernels and grinned. "I'd say God heard your prayers, all right, Uncle."

"Come on, let's show you," Roger said, motioning for his nephew to follow. He led him to the exact place where he'd found the corn. "It all happened right here. Here's where I prayed and here's where I find this ear of corn."

"Well, sir, I think you best be thinking about a way you can preserve that corn, don't you?" Paul said, taking the cob in his hand once more and running his fingertips gently over the top of the bright hard kernels. "Because I've never seen anything like it in my life."

"I know," Roger said. "If you ask me, I'd say that right there is a piece of corn hand-designed by God himself. And for some reason God in his infinite wisdom has chosen to give it to me."

"What you need is some kind of frame, Uncle; then you can make sure to keep it safe and somewheres nearby," Paul said. "That way if you ever need a reminder that God hears your prayers, it'll be as close as the next room."

"Well, I'll tell you what, Paul," Roger said. An idea was brewing in Roger's head. "I believe I'll do that and I believe something else, too. Every time anyone comes around the house I'm going to make it my job to share with them the story of the corn and the answered prayer. Because it ain't nothin' special about the corn but for the fact that God himself has made it known that he hears our prayers and he does indeed answer us. And that's something worth sharing."

Years later, not long before Roger died, he called Paul to his house and gently handed him the corn with the cross of red kernels.

"You're a farmer, Paul, and you understand how close we came to losing everything if it hadn't been for that rain," Roger said. His voice was weak, and it had been some time since he'd been able to tend to his farm.

"Now I want you to have the corn, but you gotta promise me

something. Please tell as many people as you can about what happened that summer; how God heard me and answered my prayer. And how he even gave me a sign so that I'd know how much he loves me. Tell the people, will you, Paul?"

Paul took the corn carefully from his uncle.

"Well, sir, that's mighty nice of you, but I couldn't take this ear of corn out of your family."

Roger raised one very thin hand. "Now, Paul, you're not taking the corn, I'm giving it. There's a difference. I'm doing it now, while I'm alive, so's there won't be any fight over what my intentions are.

"And you're the only one what'll understand enough to tell the story the right way. Now do as I say and take it home."

"Well, Uncle, I'd be honored," Paul said finally. "And I'll share your story with whoever wants to hear it."

Paul has kept his word, and since 1970 he has shared the story with the congregations of more than twenty churches, never accepting donations for his effort.

"This isn't about money. As a matter of fact, the man who set this ear of corn in plastic and preserved it didn't charge Uncle Roger a dime," Paul likes to say when he finishes telling the story of his uncle, the corn, and God. "He took one look at that corn and told my uncle he couldn't think of a way to put a price tag on what was so clearly God's handiwork."

Miracle in Leipzig

$\mathcal{I}$t was a cold winter day in early 1944, and Trautel Wagner had made plans to attend the opera with her longtime friend and classmate, Liesel Wolf. The girls, both nineteen, had grown up in Leipzig, Germany, and enjoyed the cultural advantages of living in a big city.

There was just one thing that bothered Trautel that day: Her mother did not want to join her and her friend. Trautel had done everything possible to convince her to go, and it saddened Trautel to see how strongly her mother's mind was made up. Trautel hated to see her stay home alone, and after all, culture was a way of life in Germany. Now that World War II was drawing to an end, people were beginning to venture out in large numbers to spend a day at the opera or an evening at the theater.

Trautel and her mother loved Leipzig, even if their family had seen such a great deal of tragedy there. Leipzig was steeped in culture, with a heritage that rivaled any center for the arts. Leibniz and Richard Wagner were born there, and great musicians including Bach and Mendelssohn had performed in Leipzig. A city with several hundred thousand people, it was also responsible for the production of steel, chemicals, textiles, toys, and other goods.

In the early 1940s, operas and ballets were a way of life for the people of Leipzig, despite the occasional bombing raids. But until that winter, Trautel and her mother—or Muttel, as Trautel often fondly called her—had been careful to avoid spending too much time in public because of the danger.

"Please be careful, dear," Trautel's mother, Ida, advised before she left that morning. "And watch out for the raids. If you hear the sirens, take shelter as fast as you can."

Trautel nodded, her dark-brown hair swinging easily around her shoulders. "Yes," she said, stooping to kiss her mother on the cheek. "Now Muttel, you're sure you won't come with us?"

"No, not this time. I am tired." Her mother nestled into the family's aging ottoman and tightened a shawl around her shoulders. "It is too cold for my bones today."

Trautel slipped into a thick jacket and waved good-bye, wondering if there weren't other reasons why her mother would want to stay home from the opera. Lately she seemed afraid to go out of the house, and Trautel could understand her reasons.

The string of tragedies that had touched the Wagner family began long before the war. In 1936, Trautel's brother, Karlheinz, had been killed when he and his friends were jumping from a hayloft one day and he misjudged his jump, landing headfirst on a patch of cement. For three days in the hospital he fought to stay alive before dying of massive brain injuries. He had been twelve, a gentle boy who loved his family dearly, and there were days when Trautel still hurt from the pain of missing him.

Five years later her father, Karl, died suddenly of a massive heart attack. He was only forty-eight years old. By that time Germany had begun to change and there was palpable tension in every major city—tension that only grew to engulf the population and finally culminate in World War II.

Together Trautel and her mother struggled to survive, learning with each passing week the names of more friends and relatives who had been killed in the war. There were many times when Ida would pull Trautel close to her and hold her tightly for several seconds.

"I have only you, my child," she would say. "We have only each other."

Although mother and daughter were rarely apart, that winter Trautel and Liesel had finally begun venturing into the opera halls and other cultural centers, trying to lead more normal lives. Ida could understand their desire to get out; after all, they were young girls and their life had been austere and dismal for such a long time. Besides, the bomb raids were growing less and less frequent; if a problem arose, there were bomb shelters scattered between the Wagners' apartment and the opera hall.

Trautel knew she could not sit at home waiting forever for a safe world outside. But she also understood her mother's fears as she left that morning. With everything the Wagner family had been through, it was possible her mother simply couldn't bear the terrifying thought of being in a public place when the air raid sirens began to scream their warning.

Trautel shut the front door behind her and walked briskly to Liesel's apartment, which was only a few blocks away. There, Liesel bid her parents good-bye, and the two friends walked several blocks to meet up with the streetcar. They climbed aboard, paid the fare, and found seats, all the time talking animatedly about how exciting it was to finally get out and what a thrill it would be to see the opera.

After a ten-minute ride the streetcar slowed to a stop. The two friends climbed out and walked the remaining three blocks to the theater. Animation and high spirits buzzed in the air as patrons filled the theater and prepared for the opera to begin. Trautel and Liesel found their seats and waited.

When the lights went down Trautel closed her eyes for a moment and prayed silently. Her faith in God was strong, and she often spoke to him the way she might speak to someone sitting beside her. Her prayer was a comforting habit. As far as Trautel was concerned, God truly was beside her at all times—at least in spirit.

"So far, so good, God," she prayed without making a sound. "No air raid sirens. Almost as if there never was a war at all. But if the bombs come, please protect me, God. Help me make it back to my mother. She needs me, God. I'm all she has left."

The opera was brilliant and emotionally moving—it swept Trautel away to another time and place when so much sorrow could not even be imagined. With a surge of emotion, she thought of her brother and her father as well as the friends and neighbors she had lost over the years, and she dabbed at her tears as the performance ended. When the house lights came up, she and Liesel made their way through the theater to the exit. Chatting about the performance, the girls sauntered arm in arm toward the streetcar, and leaped aboard when it pulled up to them.

"I can't wait to get home and tell Muttel about the opera," Trautel said. "Wasn't it wonderful?"

"I just wish it hadn't ended so soon." Liesel smiled at her friend, and Trautel grinned. "I wonder if we'll ever get to wear dresses like those."

Trautel laughed, remembering the fancy costumes worn by the lead opera singers. "Not any time soon, I don't think."

Trautel was happy riding alongside her longtime friend. Through all the tragedies there had always been a sense of comfort knowing Liesel was there for her. The girls had known each other nearly all their lives, and were almost like sisters. As the streetcar headed toward their apartments, the girls continued chatting, making new plans for the days to come.

Then without warning, just three minutes into their journey, the serenity of the afternoon was severed by the piercing wail of the air-raid sirens. Instantly the streetcar skidded to a halt.

"Please exit and go directly to the nearest bomb shelter," the conductor announced over the public-address system. "Exit immediately."

All around the girls, a strangely organized panic gripped the city as people began to run for the shelters, clutching the hands of young children and holding their parcels tightly to their bodies. Bomb shelters were located throughout the city, and clearly marked for this type of emergency.

"Hurry," Liesel demanded, grabbing her friend's hand and running across the street. As they ran, Trautel's eyes flashed up at the sky and she heard the distant sound of fighter planes approaching. Ahead the girls saw people streaming into one of the shelters. Still holding hands, they began running toward the entrance.

"Get inside!" someone shouted.

"Fast!" another voice urged.

Trautel and Liesel picked up their pace—with the planes drawing dangerously near, they flew into the shelter and found a seat among the anxious crowd. The brick and cement of the underground cavern were particularly cold, and Trautel began shivering as she closed her eyes and listened to the planes that were now directly overhead.

"It'll be okay, Trautel," Liesel whispered, squeezing her friend's hand.

Trautel nodded, her eyes still closed. Bomb shelters protected people by preventing death and injury caused by the outer blast of an explosion. People inside were safer than they were in the street—unless the shelter took a direct hit.

Trautel, Liesel, and the other people in the shelter heard the faint whistling sound of bombs being dropped in the distance. The ground beneath the girls feet shuddered from the impact. Somewhere in the city buildings were being destroyed, people killed. Trautel squeezed her eyes tightly together and tears trickled down her cheeks. *God,* she prayed, *please let my mother be okay. Please let me get home to her.*

For a long two minutes bombs whistled through the air around the city as the people in the shelter clung to each other and wept in fear. Trautel and Liesel huddled together, knowing that bombs might easily have fallen in their neighborhood since their apartments were so close to the city. Trautel hoped her mother had made it safely to the apartment building's basement bomb shelter. And she felt so strongly now that she'd do anything to be by her mother's side.

The bombs continued to fall, and Trautel clenched her fists, struggling to control the panic that welled up inside her. Never in her life had she felt more frightened, and she prayed desperately that God would help her survive.

Finally the sound of the bombers grew more and more distant, and the people packed into the shelter sighed with relief. The raid was over. Instantly, Trautel was overcome by the need to rush out of the shelter, almost as if the decision were out of her control. She remembered her prayer and how she had asked God to allow her to return home safely to her mother.

Suddenly she stood up.

"Trautel, where are you going?" Liesel's voice sounded panic-stricken.

"We need to leave, Liesel," Trautel commanded, her face contorted in fear. "I just have a feeling that we have to get home right now."

Liesel shook her head furiously. "I won't do it, and you can't either. The planes always come back a second time."

"We'll be safe," Trautel insisted. "We'll run home, and then we can be in the bomb shelters with our families. Come on!"

"No! I'm not going anywhere," Liesel said.

"Then I'm going without you. I *have* to get home, Liesel."

"Please, Trautel, stay with me. Don't go yet."

"I don't want to leave you, but I have to get to Muttel."

Tears flooded Liesel's eyes. "What if something happens to you?"

"I'll be all right. Look for me after you get home."

Trautel took her friend's hands once more and squeezed them between her own. "I'll be fine. Really."

Liesel smiled nervously and nodded. "You're not mad that I won't go?"

"Of course not. I'll see you tonight."

Liesel watched Trautel turn away and head toward the exit. There were more than two hundred people crammed into the shelter, and it took some maneuvering before Trautel reached the stairs and began climbing them.

"Girl, you cannot go."

Trautel wheeled around and saw a well-dressed man moving toward her. Quickly she shook her head. "Sir, I must go. My mother waits for me at home."

The man clutched Trautel's elbow tightly. "The bombers will be back. It is not safe to leave. You would be a fool to set foot on the streets so soon."

Trautel pictured her mother frantically waiting, worried that her daughter might lay dead in the streets of the city. She yanked her arm from the man and despite the screams of protest from several others in the shelter, she ran up the stairs, tore open the heavy door, and dashed into the street. All around, rubble lay in heaps, and she could hear injured people moaning from underneath the ruins of buildings. The raid had been extensive, and Trautel prayed again that her mother would be unharmed—actually seeing the new devastation only increased her panic.

Tightening her coat around her waist, she began running home, estimating that it could be as much as forty minutes before she reached the apartment building where they lived. At first the air remained still, but after twenty minutes, when Trautel was moving as fast as she could, she again heard the very distant sound of the bombers. The man in the shelter had been right; the planes were returning for a second raid. There would be no point in turning back toward the shelter, and she did not see another one nearby. All Trautel could do was pray again that she might make it home safely. Then, summoning her remaining strength, she kept running as fast as she could.

The planes were approaching more quickly now, and Trautel could feel her heart pounding as she forced her legs to keep pumping. She was ten minutes from home when the first bombs began dropping on the city. The impact knocked her to her knees, but she got up quickly and continued running. Five minutes passed as the planes flew overhead and circled around the heart of Leipzig. Then once more the bombers turned in unison and retreated from the area.

Breathlessly, Trautel turned the corner and saw ahead that her house was still intact. She ran with all her remaining strength up the walkway and into the building, where she raced down the stairs to the basement shelter.

"Trautel!" Her mother rushed to meet her, wrapping her arms around the girl. "You're alive."

"Muttel! Oh, Muttel, yes!" Trautel gasped for breath. "I was in the shelter but I couldn't stay. When the bombs stopped I ran home."

Ida's face paled. "Where is Liesel?"

"She stayed, Muttel. She was afraid, so I came by myself."

"You could have been killed, darling. You must always wait a long time before it is safe to leave the shelters."

Trautel nodded, fresh tears filling her eyes. "But I was so worried about you. I didn't want us to be apart."

The rest of the afternoon, mother and daughter huddled together in the shelter, and later when it was safe, in their upstairs apartment. They wondered how much damage had been done, how many lives lost, as Trautel told her mother every detail of the day and how frightened she had been when the sirens went off. As evening fell, Trautel grew silent, concerned about Liesel and wondering if she too had made it home safely.

Finally, the following morning, one of their neighbors stopped by with a report. Many buildings had been damaged and several people had been killed on the street after not making it on time to the shelters.

"But the worst tragedy of all, dear women, was the shelter near the theater," the neighbor said, hanging his head sadly.

Trautel's eyes grew wide and she felt that her heart would stop. She and Liesel had been in that shelter and hadn't known of any problem. "What is it, sir? What happened?"

The man shook his head sadly. "It happened during the second raid." He looked up and his eyes were damp. "A phosphorous bomb landed at the entrance of the shelter and began spewing sparks at the people below. Clothes caught fire and people burned. Fire spread through the shelter and there was a panic as people tried to get out the back exit. Dozens were trampled to death. There are only a few survivors."

The blood disappeared from Trautel's face and she turned deathly pale. The man lived in the building and knew Liesel and her family. "Sir, do you know about Liesel? She was in that shelter."

"I'm sorry, Trautel, she didn't make it. She was trampled under the crowd of people trying to get away from the fire."

Falling slowly to her knees, Trautel dropped her head in her hands as the impact of the man's news hit her full force. Her dear friend, Liesel, gone. The truth was almost too much to bear. She thought about the crowded shelter, the man who had warned her to stay inside. The women and children and all the others who had yelled at her not to go. Then she pictured Liesel, refusing to leave. How many of them were dead?

She reached up for her mother's hands and wept for her dead friend.

"She's gone, Muttel, my dear Liesel," Trautel sobbed. "I would have been killed alongside her if I'd stayed. Why didn't she come with me, Muttel?"

Ida's own tears streamed down her cheeks. "She did the right thing by staying, dear, you know that. No one could have known what was about to happen."

"I left because of you, Muttel. I prayed that God would let me make it back to you and he did."

The neighbor man whispered softly, "You have been spared, Trautel. God must have been listening."

Trautel cried out then, wracked with the loss of her dearest friend. Finally, when several minutes had passed and her sobbing had subsided, she looked up through red swollen eyes first at the neighbor and then at her mother.

"Not every time does life go as we would have it," she said. "Even for God's people. We have lost so much, and now we have lost Liesel. Certainly we have known death and we have known pain."

A sob caught in Trautel's throat and she forced herself to continue. "But still God loves and certainly he listens. He brought me home to you, Muttel. So that even in our pain we can be sure he is listening."

The Man from Heaven

*W*enonah Faulk sat stiffly in the chair beside her mother's bed at the Wood County Nursing Home in Bowling Green, Ohio, and watched a dozen birds fluttering outside the window.

"You know what they say about birds, don't you?" the sixty-seven-year-old Wenonah asked softly, turning toward her own daughter, Patti, who had joined her that afternoon.

"No, Mom, what do they say?"

"When birds gather outside the window of someone who's sick, it means the Lord is ready to call them home."

Wenonah held her mother's hand and stroked the wrinkled skin gently. Her mother, Mary, was eighty-six and in a coma. Doctors didn't expect her to live out the week.

"I love you, Mother," Wenonah said as tears threatened to spill onto her cheeks. Then she gazed up, closing her eyes as if to shut out the pain of death. "Dear Lord, help me accept this. Help me to let my mother go home to you."

They waited nearly an hour until it was time for dinner, and when the elderly woman showed no signs of responding, Wenonah and Patti rose from their seats and slowly left the room.

"I'll be coming back tomorrow," Wenonah said as the two women walked out toward their cars in the parking lot.

"I'll be here too, Mom," Patti said. "I'll meet you here after lunch."

Wenonah drove home without playing music on the car stereo. The sadness she felt demanded silence rather than the sounds of carefree music. Wenonah sighed and thought about her mother's decline. Two years earlier the woman had been in good health, living independently in Toledo, Ohio. Then she began struggling to manage on her own, and finally she had agreed to come live with Wenonah and her husband, Ralph, in Bowling Green.

"I don't want to be a bother to you," she had told Wenonah upon her arrival. "You just go about your business and I'll be just fine."

The beauty of the situation was that Mary stuck by her words and never imposed on the life Wenonah and Ralph led. Mary had a sweet disposition and a happy outlook that was contagious to those around her. Many afternoons she would sit outside watching Wenonah work on her flower garden or making conversation with Ralph.

Two years passed quickly, and it seemed Mary might live to be a hundred.

Then in mid-1987, she moved in with Patti so Wenonah and Ralph could take a two-week vacation to Boston. During the visit, the older woman began having a series of mini-strokes, and Wenonah was called back home when her mother was admitted to the hospital and placed in intensive care.

Two days into her hospital stay, a nurse entered Mary's room and accidentally gave her the wrong medication. The drug slowed Mary's heart and brain activity and sent her into a deep coma.

The next day the doctor was honest with Wenonah about what had happened.

"The nurse will be required to stay away from the hospital for two weeks without pay and she will be admonished," he said gently. "Still, it was an accident and one that any of us might have made."

"What does it mean for my mother?" Wenonah asked anxiously. "When will she come out of the coma?"

The doctor sighed. "That's just it, Mrs. Faulk. Because of her condition and her age, she might not come out of it. I expect she might go downhill rather rapidly at this point."

Wenonah nodded, clutching Ralph's hand and trying not to cry. "But if she comes out of it today or tomorrow, she still might make a recovery. Is that right?"

"I don't think it's likely, Mrs. Faulk. I'm trying to be as honest as possible."

When her mother remained in the coma for four days, the hospital staff decided there was nothing more they could do for her. At that point Wenonah made arrangements for her mother to be transferred to the Wood County Nursing Home.

"Mother, I hate to have you living away from us when you're feeling so sick," she would say during her daily visits to the nursing home. "But the doctors and nurses can help you here much better than I can at home. I hope you understand, Mother. I love you."

Eventually two weeks passed and now, as Wenonah drove home, she felt terribly cheated. Her mother had been healthy, spry, and witty until this incident. She might have had years left if that nurse hadn't administered the wrong medication.

Wenonah sighed aloud. She was doing her best to avoid blaming the nurse. "Lord, help me to understand why this has happened," she prayed softly. "It doesn't seem fair that Mother should be cheated of her last years of life after she's been such an inspiration to me and touched so many people."

When Wenonah got home it was nearly dusk, and she realized that Ralph was still out golfing with his friends. She set her purse on the counter and thought how cold and lonely the house felt. Just three weeks earlier they'd had company over for dinner and her mother had been doing fine. Now she lay at death's doorstep, and Wenonah struggled to make sense of the situation. How quickly and irrevocably life could change.

"I need to get outside before I work myself into a full-blown depression," Wenonah said to herself. She found her gardening gloves and pulled them over her hands, intent on pruning the dead flowers from her beautiful garden that ran alongside the fence in the front yard.

She was working steadily among the flowers, still wrestling with the unfairness of her mother's situation, when she heard a man's voice nearby.

"My, your flowers are so lovely," he said.

Wenonah looked up and saw, standing on the sidewalk, a tall man holding the leash of a beautiful little dog. Wenonah smiled sadly. Her mother loved dogs and she certainly would have enjoyed this one. Wenonah would have to tell her about it on her next visit.

"Thank you," Wenonah said, leaning back on her heals and looking up into the man's face. She had lived in the neighborhood for thirty-five years, but had never seen this person before. Wenonah glanced back down at her flowers and frowned.

"They aren't as pretty as they could be if I had more time to take care of them," she said. "It's just that my mother's sick. She's in a nursing home."

The man gazed at Wenonah kindly, and she felt that there seemed to be something unearthly about him. He waited for Wenonah to continue.

"She was given the wrong medication and now she's dying. I want to be there as much as possible."

She looked at the man, and was embarrassed to feel tears welling up in her eyes again. This man was a stranger and here she was telling him all her problems.

"Don't worry about your mother," the man said, his voice strong and gentle. "God is in control."

Wenonah wiped an errant strand of hair from her forehead and brushed the dirt off her gloves. How strange that someone she didn't know would offer such words of wisdom. The man continued to stand nearby, watching her closely.

"Sir, where do you live?" she finally asked.

The man said nothing, but only pointed upward. Instinctively, Wenonah's eyes followed the direction he was pointing, and she looked toward the sky. When she looked back down, the man and his dog were gone. There was no sign of them anywhere along the street, and it seemed there was no way they could have vanished so quickly.

Wenonah was shocked. She thought back over the conversation she had shared with the man, and she realized that she hadn't seen him arrive. He had just appeared with words of encouragement and then disappeared.

God is in control, he had said. Wenonah pondered the truth in the man's words, and found that as the evening passed she felt less burdened.

The next morning, Wenonah received a phone call from the nursing home.

"Mrs. Faulk, you'll want to come down as quickly as possible," the administrator said. "Your mother has died very peacefully in her sleep."

Wenonah shut her eyes as one hand flew to her mouth. Nothing could have prepared her for the truth, and she felt a sob catch in her throat. Then, before she could give in to the sorrow that threatened to consume her, Wenonah remembered the man in the garden. A sense of peace came over her, and suddenly she knew her prayers had been answered. She told the administrator that she'd be down in a few minutes. Then she bowed her head.

"Dear God," she whispered through her tears. "I understand now. There are no accidents where you're concerned. Mother didn't die because of that nurse or the medication; she died because you were ready to bring her home. Just like the man said, you are in control. I understand that better now, Lord. And I thank you."

ANSWER ELEVEN:

Runaway Rig on Grocer Grade?

$\mathcal{D}$ick Dolphin had been driving trucks for thirty-seven years, and was known for being nearly fanatical about safety. Regardless of the time it cost him, he would not start his engine without a thorough safety check before each and every trip. This was especially true on holidays, when the roads were packed with vacationing drivers. Memorial Day weekend 1984 was no exception.

Over the years Dick had seen ruined rigs lying on the side of the road, and he knew of drivers who had died or killed others when something mechanical on their trucks had failed.

"Safety checks can mean the difference between life and death," Dick had often told his wife, Mary, before setting out on one of his many trips. Mary worried about his safety constantly, and Dick knew she appreciated the extra attention he paid to making sure his equipment was in good order.

"It makes it better knowing how careful you are," she had said more than once. "But all the safety checks in the world don't always make a difference. Something can still go wrong, Dick. Please be careful."

Dick had driven for UPS for two decades before taking an early retirement and agreeing to drive for an asphalt company in Las Vegas, Nevada. The work involved transporting 380-degree liquid asphalt in insulated tank trailers from Santa Maria, California, to the bulk plant in Las Vegas.

Carrying hot liquid asphalt was very different from carrying parcels and packages across the country. Dick knew if he were ever to have an accident while pulling the liquid asphalt, the results could be horrific. If anything punctured the insulated tanks and caused even a small amount of the molten, tar-like substance to land on a person, it could burn that person to death in minutes.

The trip between Santa Maria and Las Vegas took eight hours, and Dick ran the route as often as three times a week, pulling tons of the liquid asphalt each time. He could afford no mistakes.

On Saturday morning of that Memorial Day weekend, Dick was especially anxious to get home. His son, Richard, would be passing through Las Vegas on his way to Idaho, and would be there that evening and through the next day. Dick watched as the last of the steaming liquid asphalt was loaded into the tanks on his double trailer.

Despite his desire to get on the road, Dick did not take short-cuts when it came to making his safety checks. Paying careful attention to every detail, Dick made his way around the rig to double-check each valve connection. When he was sure they were tight, he checked the tires and hoses.

Finally, when the trailers were filled, Dick removed the pipe tilt-riser and tightened the hatch. According to the scales at the loading station, the entire rig weighed 79,540 pounds, barely under the eighty-thousand-pound limit for tractor-trailers in California.

Before taking off, Dick again walked around his rig re-checking his equipment, especially the brakes. His drive back to

Las Vegas included several hills, and he wanted to be sure his brakes were in perfect condition before setting off.

Finally, satisfied with the safety of his rig, Dick climbed into the driver's seat and drove to Highway 166, a two-lane road that curved around Twitchell Reservoir, up across Los Padres National Forest, and eventually down through the Cuyama River valley.

Dick hummed a carefree tune as he made his way, glad for the warm day. Warm weather always helped maintain the intense heat of the asphalt, keeping it in a liquid form. This would help make unloading an easy job when he arrived at the plant in Las Vegas later that evening.

Shifting gears, Dick began climbing the Elkhorn Hills. As he neared the top, approaching Grocer Grade, he checked his gauges again to be sure he had plenty of air pressure for the steep eight-mile trip down into the small town of Maricopa. The air was fine. Dick began down the grade and felt the gravitational pull on his truck.

The downhill speed limit on the grade was thirty-five miles per hour for trucks, so Dick shifted again, placing the truck's transmission into an even lower gear that would help maintain the proper speed. The first three miles of the grade consisted of a series of switchback turns, and Dick maneuvered his rig gracefully around each corner without incident.

He cleared the final sharp turn, and began an equally steep five-mile stretch through rolling farmland. At this point in the two-lane highway there were no more switchbacks, just wide curves from there to the bottom of the mountain.

As Dick straightened his truck out and prepared for the final five miles of the grade, he noticed that the rig had gradually begun gaining speed. Instead of thirty-five, he was now going forty, and his speedometer was creeping higher.

I'm losing the brakes, he thought. Instinctively he reached for the gearshift, knowing that a lower gear would assist the brakes by holding back the engine. But as soon as he began downshifting he realized something had gone terribly wrong with his engine.

Each time he attempted to shift into the lower gear, the transmission would pop back out, refusing to shift. Dick knew what was happening; it was a truck driver's worst nightmare. The truck was traveling too fast for the transmission to take the pressure of a lower gear without some help from the brakes. Dick continued to apply the brakes as much as possible, but he could feel them getting hot and less effective with each passing second.

The speedometer climbed past fifty as Dick pushed the brake pedal to the floor, making one last desperate attempt to slow the rig. Instead, the tractor and its two-part trailer began racing uncontrollably down the grade.

Concentrate, Dick thought. He forced himself to block out everything except what was directly on the road ahead of him. From his vantage point far above the road Dick could see dozens of cars on the two-lane road ahead. And there were still four miles of steeply graded road left.

Suddenly Dick was overcome by a wave of panic. If he lost control or crashed into another vehicle, the trailer tanks would surely burst open and spray deadly liquid asphalt across the people and cars in its path. The impact alone would be enough to cause numerous serious and fatal injuries.

Dick felt an overwhelming urge to protect the lives of other drivers around him, all of whom were unaware of his predicament. But for the first time in his truck-driving career he was completely out of control and none of his carefulness could help him. After all, he had checked every possible aspect of his rig before setting out that morning, and nothing had been amiss. This was what Mary had worried about so often. His truck had inexplicably failed him.

Dick was not a man who spent much time thinking about God. But at that instant he had nowhere else to turn.

"Please, God," he prayed, "I need you to help me. There's innocent people here who are going to be killed if you don't get me through this. Help me to make the right choices and get me to the bottom of the hill, God. I can't do it alone."

Instantly, as if someone had flipped a switch, the cars and obstacles that lay ahead seemed to be moving toward him in slow motion. The panic disappeared and Dick could once again think clearly, almost as if a heavenly presence was in the cab guiding him down the hill.

In less than a minute, the truck reached seventy miles per hour—the maximum listed on the speedometer—and Dick could feel it continuing to gain speed. He looked ahead and saw that he was quickly approaching the back of two cars in his lane. In the other lane, a car was coming toward him. He had no choice but to pass the cars in his way and hope he'd get back over again without hitting the oncoming car.

Help me make it, God, he prayed silently. Then he slid his rig around the cars in his path and jerked the truck back into his lane of traffic, missing the approaching car by only a few feet.

"Thank you," he whispered. But he immediately found another obstacle lay in his path. This time it was a short line of three cars, then some space, and then another tractor-trailer rig. Although his speedometer was stuck at seventy, Dick knew he must be traveling much faster than that, and still he was picking up speed. He needed to act quickly or he would mow down the cars in his path—and the people in them.

Without any trace of the panic that had gripped him only moments before, he swung the rig across the center line, sped past the three cars, and pulled back deftly into his lane behind the truck. Dick glanced at the oncoming traffic and saw that there were numerous cars headed his way, more than there had been before. He would not be able to pass the big rig in front of him under these conditions. Suddenly Dick was left with no means of escape.

By then Dick estimated that he was careening down the road at about eighty-five miles per hour. If he hit the much slower-moving truck in front of him, they would both be destroyed in a sea of liquid asphalt.

"Help me, God!" he cried aloud. "Help!"

At that instant he glanced to his right and saw that the shoulder had widened considerably. Dick estimated that the shoulder space between the road and an adjacent ditch might be wide enough for him to pass without flipping the trailers.

Seeing no other choice, Dick steered slightly toward the right and sent his rig soaring onto the gravel-covered shoulder. The tractor and double trailer both bounced and swayed, on the verge of tumbling. Dust rose ominously into the air, and hoses and other unloading equipment flew off the sides of the trailers.

Dick passed the other truck, hoping the uneven shoulder might slow his speed, but instead the rig continued to move faster. Just then Dick remembered that he would be coming up on a culvert— that meant there would be no shoulder for a stretch of the roadway. Not knowing how much shoulder space he had left, Dick worked the tractor back onto the roadway, all the while praying that the trailers wouldn't overturn. Every bit of the rig shook and shuddered as Dick straightened it back onto the road, but the truck managed to remain upright and Dick again concentrated on what lay ahead.

He had been in this white-knuckle situation for less than five minutes, but it seemed like an eternity. Ahead there was one final curve in the road, and Dick could see a single car between him and the bottom of the hill. On his right, the shoulder had disappeared, and now there were only deep ditches on either side of the highway. Whatever he did, he would have to stay on the road or risk death.

Dick assessed the oncoming traffic, and saw a single car that prevented him from passing the vehicle in front of him. Since he had exhausted most of his pressurized air while pumping the brakes, his air horn had become useless. There would be no way even to warn the car in front of him about the impending collision.

"Help me, God!" Dick prayed again. Desperation crept into his voice despite the calm that still prevailed in his mind. "Please help me!"

At once, the oncoming car pulled off the road and stopped,

allowing Dick to swing into that lane and pass the last car in his path.

By that time six minutes had passed, and Dick estimated that his speed had increased to more than one hundred miles an hour. Maricopa lay just ahead of him; again Dick prayed that he wouldn't hurt anyone.

At the bottom of the grade, the highway curved to the right alongside a small hamburger stand, which stood just left of the road. It was 11 a.m., and because of the holiday weekend an early lunch crowd milled about, ordering food and taking it back to their cars. Dick's mind could not help going to what would happen if he tried to make the curve and lost control of his rig. He could wipe out the hamburger stand and everyone near it.

The risk was too great, and in an instant he decided to continue straight onto a road that led past a convenience store and ended a block later, where it intersected with another highway. If Dick could somehow make it to that point without hitting anyone, he could cross the highway, drive up a cement curbing, and onto a dirt area nestled between a row of houses and an irrigation ditch.

Dick continued to concentrate. Any error would be fatal to someone.

Struggling to keep control of the rig, Dick soared off the main highway and continued straight ahead. At the same instant a driver leaving the convenience store pulled out in front of him and headed for the stop sign. Traffic was approaching in the oncoming lane to the left, and a steep ditch ran along the edge of the road on the right. Once again there was nothing Dick could do but pray.

"God, if he stops we're both dead," Dick whispered. "Please help me."

The car barely slowed for the stop sign before turning left, the driver unaware of the mortal danger he had been in or even of the existence of the speeding truck bearing down on him. With the way clear once more, Dick prayed again that no other driver would cross in front of him. Then he careened past the convenience store and rocketed through the stop sign.

He saw that the house to the left had yard-sale items spread out on the lawn; across the street children were playing in their yards and neighbors were out visiting. He thought of the hot liquid asphalt and how far it could spray if one of the trailers burst open at a hundred miles an hour. Then he aimed his rig directly between a house on the left and the ditch on the right. The front tires of his tractor hit the four-inch curbing with a sickening thud.

Suddenly the entire rig twisted toward the house on the left and became airborne. Still soaring through the air, the trailers separated themselves and fell to the ground. The tractor finally came down 250 feet away from the road, landing on its wheels and sliding out of control toward the house.

Yard-sale wares were spread out across the lawn, but miraculously, there wasn't a person in the rig's path. The cab wiped out used books, kitchenware, and clothing as it skidded through a wall in the house and finally came to a shuddering stop. The eaves from the roof had torn through Dick's windshield and rested just inches from his forehead.

The impact jammed Dick's fingers, which were still tightly wrapped around the steering wheel, and his ear was cut from hitting his head against the left window. But otherwise he was unharmed. It had been just under six minutes since he'd lost his brakes nine miles back at the top of the grade.

"Thank you, God," he said, squeezing his eyes shut.

Then, remembering the hot liquid asphalt, he climbed down from his rig. The trailer tanks had landed fifty feet away near a tree at the far end of the house. Miraculously, they were intact.

Dick walked to the front doorstep and rang the bell, praying again that no one inside the house had been harmed. At that moment a woman who lived in the house across the street approached him.

"Are you all right?" she asked, glancing at his cab, which jutted strangely from her neighbor's house.

"Fine," Dick said. "Where are the people who live here? I'm worried they might be trapped in that room."

"It's the strangest thing," the woman said. "They were having a big yard sale and people were all over their place shopping around. Then about a few minutes ago they were called away for some sort of emergency. They left everything in the yard and asked me to keep an eye on it from across the street."

The woman's eyes widened as she looked at the trailers lying alongside the tree fifty feet away. "Just a few minutes ago their little girl was playing right in that spot," she said, clearly astonished. "She's only four. She would never have seen you coming."

Dick closed his eyes again and breathed another prayer of thanks. Remembering each near-miss incident in the past few minutes, and how many times his prayers for safety had been answered, Dick was speechless. He moved slowly toward the cab of his truck and pulled his things from inside. As he walked away, focused on finding a telephone, one of the tanks suddenly split open, sending tons of the intensely hot liquid asphalt spilling across the lawn, covering the yard and the place where Dick had been standing only seconds before.

Dick stared mesmerized at the flowing asphalt, and shouted warnings toward passersby who were beginning to gather at the scene. "Stay away!" he screamed. "That stuff's so hot it'll kill you."

After the people had moved back a safe distance, a man approached Dick.

"I was driving the car that pulled over," he said in a shocked voice. "The one coming toward you. I didn't know you were having trouble until I saw you pass and I could tell you were going too fast."

"Why did you stop?" Dick asked, puzzled.

"Something just told me to pull over," he replied. "After I realized what was happening, I had to turn back down the mountain and see if you were all right."

Chill bumps broke out across Dick's arms and back. "I didn't have anywhere to go," he said. "If you hadn't pulled over, someone would have been killed."

Dick thanked the man and then, thinking of how he had nearly been covered with liquid asphalt, he paused once more to thank God—this time for protecting him from burning to death.

Later that afternoon Dick phoned Mary to tell her what had happened. His voice was thick with emotion as he explained the experience.

"I asked God for help and he provided it, Mary," he told her. "There simply isn't any other way to understand it."

"How in the world did it happen, Dick?" Mary was terrified at how close her husband had come to disaster. "Didn't you check your brakes before you left?"

"Of course. But, Mary, I've learned something today. It's like you've always said, mechanical parts can fail without any warning whatsoever."

For that reason in the years that followed the ordeal on Grocer Grade, Dick always added one final item to his exhaustive list of safety checks: a simple prayer for safe travel.

The Power of Forgiveness

$\mathcal{B}$y January 1993, the hate in Lisa Lewis's heart had grown so intense, it felt as if it might actually strangle her. It hadn't always been that way.

Several years earlier, in October 1989, when Lisa and Mark Lewis bought their Canoga Park, California, condominium, it was a dream come true. The couple had planned and saved for years, hoping to one day own a home of their own, and the condo was the perfect find. They were ecstatic the day they moved in with their daughter, Jill.

They had no way of knowing the nightmare it would one day become.

The Lewises' condo was on Sherman Way, a busy street in the heart of Canoga Park, located in the San Fernando Valley east of Los Angeles. The timing of the purchase seemed perfect because home prices in the Los Angeles area climbed with each passing month and the

Lewises had gotten a good deal. They were content to enjoy their purchase and watch their investment grow.

But over the next year California slipped into a recession that seemed to freeze home prices overnight. Months passed, and the California recession grew worse. Along with it, life in much of the Los Angeles area seemed to be deteriorating. There was over-crowding, public schools were in disarray, gangs had infested the area, and graffiti began showing up everywhere.

Meanwhile, masses of people who had lived in the area all their lives were putting their homes on the market, hoping to cash in on a lifetime of equity—sometimes several hundred thousand dollars. By mid-1991, there were as many as ten homes for sale on every block throughout the Valley, and prices were falling at an average of three thousand dollars a month.

"I'm worried," Lisa told Mark one evening after Jill was in bed. "The Valley's changing and the prices are dropping. What should we do, Mark?"

Mark puzzled for a moment, not sure of his answer. He was aware of the downward trend in home prices, but he wasn't ready to pull up stakes and leave the area. He had grown up in the San Fernando Valley, and he believed it would regain its strength. He only wondered how long it would take.

"I have a good job, Lisa, and we have time to wait this thing out," he said. "Let's give it some time and see what happens."

Late that summer the Lewises lost two car stereos to the thieves in the area. In autumn a young Mexican man was killed in a drive-by shooting just outside the building that housed the Lewises' con-dominium. Lisa and Mark decided the time had come to sell. They might stay in the Valley, but they no longer felt safe on Sherman Way. When the New Year arrived, the Lewises put their condo on the market.

"We'll take a loss, but it won't be too bad," Mark told Lisa. "Let's just hope we can sell it."

There were no offers for the condo throughout winter and into spring. Then in April, in the wake of controversial and racially heated court verdicts handed down in Los Angeles, riots broke out throughout the city. Mark was managing a stereo store in Los Angeles which stocked elite home and auto sound systems. He watched in horror as rioters set fire to buildings and mayhem reigned in the streets near his store. Over the next few days several people died trying to save their businesses; others died in fires or from random gunfire. It seemed the entire city had lost all semblance of order.

Mark learned that the store he managed had indeed been looted, robbed of its entire stock of inventory. The place had been torn apart, holes punched in walls, windows broken, counters overturned.

Mark's supervisor advised him that the company would wait until after the riots to re-open, and then it would operate from the back of a truck in the parking lot since tensions in the area were still so high and the store was months away from being usable. A security guard would be posted around the clock to protect the safety of Mark and other employees.

That week Mark contacted the president of Audio Control, an elite stereo-sound-equipment distributor in Washington State. The man had been in touch with Mark before, and Mark knew the company was looking for a full-time sales representative. Fifteen minutes later he had an invitation to fly to Seattle the following week for an interview.

The Lewises' condo remained on the market, and home prices continued to fall, as Mark successfully worked his way through a string of interviews with Audio Control. Finally, in July he accepted a position with the company.

The decision was an easy one, but the move would be painful. Lisa's parents and sisters and brother all lived within three miles of their condo, and she and Mark had several close friends they'd be leaving behind.

"What about the condo?" Lisa asked. "We can't afford to have two house payments."

"We'll have to sell it soon or find renters."

The next day the couple lowered their asking price, hoping to attract a quick sale. But there were no offers, and when Mark left in August, Lisa and Jill stayed behind to show the unit until it sold.

"Don't worry," Mark said as Lisa bid him a tearful good-bye at the airport. "I can stay with my new boss until the condo sells. It'll happen soon, honey."

But August turned into September, and still there was not a single offer on the condo. Finally, the couple made plans to rent the unit so Lisa and Jill could join Mark in Washington. Lisa put an advertisement in the newspaper and waited for the calls.

"It's such a good price," Lisa told Mark when the two decided to ask $650 a month for rent. "I bet we get a hundred calls the first day."

Instead they received just two all week. The first was from an elderly lady who was no longer interested once she learned that the unit was on the second floor. The second was from a woman named Carol Grayson. She was in her early twenties, looking for a place where she and her husband, Kent, and their infant son could live affordably. Lisa showed her the condo later that afternoon.

"I really like it," Carol said softly, staring nervously at her hands. "But it's still a little bit expensive for us."

Lisa stared blankly at the woman. Two-bedroom condominiums in that area typically rented for eight hundred dollars a month—approximately the cost of the Lewises' mortgage payment.

"Carol, I think our price is very competitive," Lisa said. "There isn't anything else in that price range in the area."

Carol nodded sadly. "I know. It's just high for us."

Lisa thought a moment and had an idea. "Well, we're trying to sell the unit, as you know. How about if we charge you six hundred a month and you agree to keep the place neat and have it ready whenever realtors show it?"

Carol's face brightened. "That's a wonderful idea. I'm sure we could make things work at that price."

Lisa smiled, hoping that Mark would agree with the arrangement. "Now, about the credit report," Lisa said.

"Well," Carol interrupted, "that's something of a problem."

Lisa waited for the young woman to continue.

"See, we've been living with my folks and we really haven't established any credit just yet. But we both have jobs and believe me, we'd take great care of your condo."

Lisa thought a moment. "Why don't you fill out the application. Put the name and phone number of someone we can contact at your work and your husband's work."

Carol nodded and began filling out the application. When she finished she stood and shook Lisa's hand, smiling gratefully. "Thank you. I know you could get more for it."

"Actually, I don't have time to find out," Lisa admitted. "My husband is already working in Seattle and I need to join him. So it works out well for both of us."

The next day Lisa verified the information on the Graysons' application and cleared the situation with Mark. Then she called Carol. The woman agreed to pay the first month's rent immediately so they could move in October 1.

Carol was true to her word, and the check arrived the next morning. Three days later a moving van loaded up the Lewises belongings, and Mark found a small apartment near his office where the family could live until the condo sold. Things were working out.

But after Lisa and Jill joined Mark in Washington, weeks passed and still there was no offer on the condo. November 1 came and went with no rent check from the Graysons, and on the fifth of the month Mark contacted them by telephone. Kent answered after six rings.

"Just wanted to make sure everything was on schedule," Mark said politely. "Your rent's past due, you know."

"Yeah, well, it's in the mail," Kent snarled. "Don't worry about it."

When the envelope arrived five days later, on the tenth, Lisa opened it and found a check made out to the Department of Water and Power. She felt a pit form in her stomach. With Mark out of town at a sales conference, Lisa telephoned the Graysons that night. This time Carol answered, and Lisa could hear a television set blaring in the background.

"What?" Carol snapped.

"Uh, Carol, this is Lisa Lewis. Your check arrived today but it's made out to the power company."

"Oh, right," Carol said, and Lisa noticed that her voice sounded different, colder than it had before. "We got the checks mixed up in the mail."

There was silence for a moment. "Well, when can you send us the check? It's already ten days late, Carol."

"Listen, that's not my problem." Carol's voice rose in anger. "We'll get it to you as soon as we can. All right?"

"Okay, but don't forget the fifty-dollar late fee if it arrives after the fifteenth."

"Yeah, yeah," Carol muttered indifferently. "Whatever."

The conversation ended, and Lisa hung up the phone furious with Carol Grayson. How dare she act so rude when she was the one late on her rent! Especially after how Lisa had lowered the price to accommodate the woman.

When Mark returned, Lisa shared her concerns.

"What if it was all a big act and they never send us another rent check?" she asked. "What if I misjudged her?"

"They can't just live in our condo without paying rent, Lisa. If we don't get the check soon they'll have to leave. It's that simple."

But it wasn't that simple.

Time passed with no rent check for November, and then December. The Graysons never answered their telephone when the Lewises called, and finally Lisa contacted their realtor.

"What should we do?" Lisa asked. "They aren't paying rent and we want them out. Can we post a notice?"

The realtor sighed. "I was afraid this might happen," she said. "Lisa, I hate to tell you this, but we aren't showing your unit anymore. We can't. The place is filthy. There's dirty diapers and dishes everywhere. Their food sits in a cooler on the floor. The place actually stinks."

Lisa was livid. "Then I want them out tomorrow," she stated firmly. "Can your office post a notice on the door?"

The realtor paused uncomfortably. "Actually, there's more to it than that. You need to contact the courts and then they send someone out to post a notice."

Lisa rubbed her eyebrows in frustration as she cradled the telephone against her right shoulder. "If we do that when's the soonest they'd be out?"

"Well, although you and Mark are the owners, in California the law is on the side of the occupants—even if they haven't been paying rent. If they know about the law, it could take you a year to get them out."

"What?" Lisa shrieked. "You're kidding."

"Lisa, I worked with a couple once who spent ten thousand dollars in legal fees to get non-paying tenants out of their building. The process took ten months."

Lisa was stunned. She thanked the realtor for the information, and explained the situation to Mark that night.

"How about if we just send your brother down there with a baseball bat?" Mark suggested in frustration. Lisa's brother was six-foot-six and weighed more than three hundred pounds. Lisa smiled at the thought.

"Right now that sounds pretty good," she said with a chuckle. "But really, Mark, what are we going to do?"

Mark had no answers. Two weeks passed, and one night the Lewises received a phone call from Kent Grayson.

"Listen, we've talked to Renters' Rights and we know the situation. We can stay here a long, long time without paying a dime in rent. Nothing you can do about it."

"It's not a very responsible move, Mr. Grayson," Mark said, struggling to remain calm. "It'll ruin your credit."

Kent Grayson laughed wickedly. "Like we care about our credit rating. Can't ruin what you don't have, Mr. Lewis."

There was a click, and Mark realized that his tenant had hung up the phone. Later that night the Lewises agreed it was the worst possible situation. They were making the mortgage payment on the condo and the rent payment in Washington, home prices were still dropping, and realtors couldn't show their unit until their highly unsuitable tenants left.

By mid-January there was more bad news. The only way the Lewises could proceed against the Graysons in the eviction process was to personally attend a series of court appearances or hire an attorney to attend on their behalf. Lisa made several phone calls, and learned that attorneys charged as much as $250 for the initial eviction consultation, and hundreds of dollars for each court appearance needed throughout the process.

"It makes me furious," she told Mark that night. "I hate them for what they're doing to us. It isn't fair."

Mark held Lisa in his arms. "I guess you and Jill will have to return to Los Angeles and stay at your mom's house. Then you can make the court appearances yourself."

Lisa clenched her fists. "I hope they go to jail for this, Mark. I mean it, I really hate them."

"Hey, hey," Mark said softly. "We'll survive this, Lisa. You can't let the hate consume you."

But it did. Lisa woke up angry, and stayed that way through the day. She thought about illegal ways in which they might be able to intimidate the couple into leaving the condo. And she thought about the bad things she hoped might happen to them for the problems they were causing her and her family. She thought about the rioters and how they had ruined everything, and she hated them too. At night, she had trouble sleeping because she was so consumed with hate.

Lisa was especially upset with Carol. The young woman had put on an act, pretending to be sweet and responsible when in fact she was neither. Lisa hoped for the day when she could face the woman in person.

One afternoon, a week before she and Jill were scheduled to leave for Los Angeles, Lisa was ironing while Jill watched a children's videotape. Lisa was familiar with the storyline. It was about the Donut Repair Club, a place where people came to learn how to fix the holes in their hearts. The theme song included the words "Life without Jesus is like a donut, there's a hole in the middle of your heart."

Trying if just for a moment not to think about the problems with the Graysons, Lisa began listening to Jill's tape.

"Some people aren't kind to each other and that's pretty scary," the Donut Man was saying. "But I can think of something even scarier. It's a big, scary monster that wants to crawl into your heart. Do you know what it is?"

On the tape, several sweet-faced children shook their heads in unison.

"I'll tell you then," the Donut Man continued. "It's the monster of unforgiveness. If we let that monster in our hearts, there won't be any room left for Jesus. And that's the scariest thing of all."

Suddenly tears filled Lisa's eyes, and she set the iron upright, turning off the switch. Slowly she crossed the room and sat down, burying her face in her hands. Silently, as a flood of tears fell from her eyes, Lisa began to pray.

"Dear God, I have been filled with unforgiveness and hate so that I can almost feel it strangling me. It's like the joy and light in my life is being consumed by darkness. Truly it is like a monster and, Lord, I want it out. Forgive me for my hatred."

She sobbed softly, not wanting Jill to see her crying. Then she released her clenched fists and allowed her shoulders to relax.

"I'm giving the situation to you, God. And I'm asking you to help me forgive the Graysons for what they're doing to us."

She dried her eyes and sat further back on the sofa, savoring the peace that had come over her. For the first time in months the hate was gone. With God's help she would never let herself be consumed by hatred again.

The tape ended and Lisa laughed at the irony. The program was intended to teach Jill about God's love and forgiveness. But that day's lesson had been for her alone.

Three days passed, and the Lewises were enjoying an evening together when the telephone rang. It was their realtor.

"Lisa, you're not going to believe this," she said. "I went by the condo and the Graysons are gone. The place is cleaned out and all their mess has been removed."

Lisa was speechless, and she motioned for Mark to get on the other line. "But," Lisa stammered, "I don't understand. When did they leave?"

"According to the neighbors they must have left Wednesday night."

Mark continued the conversation as goose bumps covered Lisa's arms. Wednesday afternoon she had seen Jill's video and prayed for God to help her forgive the Graysons. Hours later they had packed up and left.

There would be more trials ahead as the Lewises worked to sell their condo, but Lisa felt blessed beyond belief.

"I gave everything over to God," she told Mark later, "and he moved mountains for us. All he wanted me to do was stop hating and start forgiving. Just like the Bible says."

When Life Changed in an Instant

*R*ain poured from the skies over the town of Buckeye, Arizona, on May 27, 1981, but Kelly Miller's future couldn't have been brighter. She was an intelligent, pretty junior at Buckeye High School with dozens of friends and a fiancé whom she loved dearly. Ted Barnes had known Kelly for quite some time, and the two planned to be married shortly after graduation, a year from that May.

There were three days of school left that rainy Monday afternoon, and Kelly was excited about having the entire summer ahead of her. But that day vacation plans would have to wait since she had to drive fifteen miles into Phoenix for her afternoon job.

Climbing into her car, she turned the key in the ignition and flipped on her windshield wipers. Reluctantly the blades skidded across her windshield, leaving bits of sun-baked rubber in their wake. Kelly sighed and ran back into the house, where her father had just arrived home from work and had telephoned Kelly's sister, who lived in another state. When they settled in for a visit, they were always on the phone for at least forty-five minutes. Kelly motioned for his attention.

"Dad, my wipers don't work and it's pouring out there," she whispered. "Can I use your car to get to work?"

Her father nodded easily, reached for the keys to his Volkswagen Bug, and tossed them to Kelly.

"Drive safe," he said, smiling at his daughter. Then he resumed his conversation.

Kelly thanked him and disappeared out the front door. Because of the weather she took surface streets toward Phoenix. The drive was uneventful until she was about three miles from home, when she noticed that her father's small car was shaking from the force of the wind. Ahead Kelly saw a stop sign and she slid her foot over to the car's brake.

Suddenly everything went black.

About the same time, Jeff Reid walked out of the auto shop where he worked to check on the weather. As he gazed toward the sky he was shocked to see a whirling funnel-shaped cloud bearing down on the roadway before him.

"Hey, guys," he shouted back toward the shop. "Come get a look at this thing."

The Phoenix area had occasionally experienced a tornado during monsoon season, but May was too early for monsoons, and the whirling windstorms of May were typically too small to do much damage. Now, as Jeff analyzed the funnel cloud headed his way, he believed it was strong enough to tear the roof off a building. Jeff knew that stretch of roadway was surrounded mainly by open fields, so there were no buildings in danger. He also knew that the danger would instead be to any cars in the funnel cloud's path.

He tore his eyes from the whirling cloud and scanned the road. It was clear of cars except for a yellow Volkswagen which was slowing to a stop directly beneath the funnel cloud. The driver, a young woman, was unaware of the narrow swirling cloud descending over her car, and Jeff waved at her frantically.

"Tornado!" he shouted.

But at that very instant the cloud engulfed the vehicle, picking it up and flipping it like a child's toy three times in midair. Jeff watched in horror as the force of the wind slammed the Volkswagen into an irrigation ditch, and then sucked it back into the air once more, before slamming it down on its wheels in the middle of a cotton field. The funnel cloud then turned indifferently and danced across the field and into the open desert, where it lost strength. In less than a minute it had disappeared completely.

"Someone call 911!" Jeff screamed at his coworkers as he raced across the street and into the field toward the battered Volkswagen. Help might be there soon, but Jeff wasn't sure it was necessary. *No one could live through that, he thought.*

Kelly tentatively opened her eyes, and saw that she was in the middle of a field of cotton. The windows of her father's Bug were gone, and her head lay limply on its side across the vehicle's back motor cover. The rest of her body lay twisted in the backseat, and her left leg was crushed between the front seat and the door. The metal where Kelly's head rested was hot from the engine beneath, and Kelly attempted to pull her head back into the car.

A searing pain burned in Kelly's back and her body remained motionless. She could not move, and terror gripped her as she heard herself scream.

"Dear God, help me!"

At that instant Jeff reached the car breathless and amazed to find the young woman alive. "Don't move, honey," he said. "Everything's going to be okay."

Kelly ignored the man and tried with all her being to move her head off the motor cover. When nothing happened, she tried to move her feet and her hands. There was no movement at all; only the feeling of intense burning in her back.

"God!" she screamed again. "Help me! Please help me!"

"Listen, stay calm," Jeff said, standing very near Kelly and moving her blond hair out of her eyes. "An ambulance is on the way. Now tell me your name and phone number and I'll call your parents."

"They're on the phone with my sister," Kelly moaned, then choked out the number. The pain was becoming unbearable, and she no longer even noticed the uncomfortably hot metal beneath her head. "Have the operator break through and get them here, please."

As Jeff disappeared with the information, two other men who had witnessed the funnel cloud pick up the Volkswagen approached and began telling Kelly she was going to be fine. As they spoke, she passed out. When Kelly regained consciousness, she could hear her father's voice.

"Kelly, honey, wake up," he said. Kelly opened her eyes and saw him standing inches from her. Nearby her mother was screaming hysterically. Tears welled in Kelly's eyes, and when she spoke her voice was weak and barely audible.

"Dad, please make Mom stop screaming," she pleaded weakly, her eyes half open.

Her father wheeled around and shouted, "You're scaring her, please, Evelyn, stop screaming." After that there was silence.

"Daddy, what happened?" Kelly whispered. "Look at your car."

"Don't worry about my car," he said, his eyes damp. "Let's take care of you."

Kelly closed her eyes once more as paramedics arrived on the scene and began working with metal cutters to free her from the nearly unrecognizable remains of her father's Volkswagen. Her limp body was strapped to a straight board, and her parents heard paramedics discussing her back injury. They hurried her into a waiting helicopter and airlifted her to nearby St. Joseph's Hospital.

My God, Evelyn prayed silently as the helicopter lifted into the air, *please don't take her from us. Please let her live.*

But a pit had formed in the mother's stomach at the sight of her daughter unable to move any part of her body. The girl who had been active all her life, athletic and graceful, a constant blur of energy, could be paralyzed. Tears filled Evelyn's eyes as she considered the devastating possibilities. Even if her daughter lived, her life would be changed forever.

When Kelly awoke she was in a hospital bed. Out of the corner of her eye, she could see screws protruding from her temples. Weights dangled from her head, and she was strapped into a device that seemed to be stretching her body. Her parents were near her bed crying, and a doctor was in the room. Kelly's eyes sought his immediately.

"Hi," she said, her voice groggy. "I'm going to be okay, right?"

"Kelly," the doctor sighed, and moved closer to her. "You need to know the truth about what happened. A funnel cloud picked up your car and slammed you onto the ground two separate times. The impact forced you headfirst into the rear windshield, breaking your back and crushing your spinal cord."

Kelly's face went white and her eyes grew watery. "So, how long until I'm better?"

"I'm sorry to have to tell you this, Kelly. You're paralyzed from the neck down. You will not walk again." Later he would tell her she'd never be able to have children.

Kelly's parents stood at her bedside, tears streaming down their faces as they watched their daughter take the news. The doctor had spoken with them the day before, and they had already had time to grieve. Now they wanted to be strong for Kelly, but it was nearly impossible.

Kelly turned her head slowly toward her parents, her eyes searching theirs. "It's a lie, it's not true," she said, her voice louder and stronger than before. "I will walk again. I'm leaving this hospital and graduating with my class. And I'm going to marry Ted."

Evelyn closed her eyes and buried her head in her husband's shoulder. He stroked his wife's hair and smiled at Kelly.

"Sweetheart, if anyone can do it, you can," he said softly.

"Not me, Dad. God," Kelly responded. "I've asked God to heal me and he will. He can do anything, you know."

Her parents nodded. "We're all praying, Kelly," her mother said. "And we'll keep praying until you can walk again. Honey, do you want us to call Ted in?"

"Please," Kelly whispered, fresh tears filling her eyes.

Tall with dark hair and serious brown eyes, Ted had been at the hospital keeping vigil for Kelly since her arrival the day before. He had listened to the doctors explain her condition, and had not yet been able to stop crying. His mind was wracked with despair as he considered their plans for the future and how they had been torn apart in an instant. He and Kelly shared a strong faith in God and attended church together. But it was difficult to see God's plan at a time like this, and he wrestled with his range of emotions.

He thought about their plans to be married and Kelly's dream of having a big family. Now she would never walk up the aisle, never bear children, and never share with him the life they had imagined. Instead there was only the harsh reality of Kelly strapped to a wheelchair every day for the rest of her life. He wondered how he would find the strength to stand by her, but he did not doubt that he would. He loved her with all his might and although their lives would not be what they had planned, he would always remain by her side.

"Ted." Evelyn interrupted his thoughts, poking her head out of Kelly's hospital room. "She's awake. She wants to see you."

Ted glanced up and wiped his eyes. Drawing a deep breath, he steadied himself and entered her room.

Kelly's eyes met his, and tears trickled onto her cheeks.

"I'm sorry," she sobbed. "Oh, Ted, I'm so sorry."

Ted moved next to her and took her lifeless hand in his, placing a finger across his lips. "Shh," he said, his voice soothing and filled with concern. He bent over and kissed her tenderly on the

lips, keeping his face inches from hers. "We'll make it throu
thing together, Kelly. Everything's going to be all right."

Kelly nodded and looked heavenward. "God will heal me, Ted.
I know he will."

Ted nodded, and his tears mingled with hers. "Don't ever stop
believing."

For three days Kelly tried desperately to move her fingers and
toes, with no success. Then on the fourth day the doctor decreased
the weight on her head, and suddenly Kelly was able to wiggle her
right leg and both arms. The doctor's eyes grew wide in amaze-
ment, and he summoned another doctor into the room.

"Look at this," he said, motioning to Kelly to move once more.
When she did, the doctor furrowed his brow and reached for her
chart.

"That's impossible," he said. "X-rays show extensive damage
to the spinal cord and a break in the vertebrae."

Kelly smiled at the doctors. "God doesn't care what the X-rays
say. He's going to heal me. I'll walk again; wait and see."

Later that week Kelly asked her mother to find her Bible, bring
it to the hospital, and read it to her. When her mother arrived she
found a passage in the Book of Psalms from the 116th chapter:

*"I love the Lord because he hears me; he listens to my prayers.
He listens to me every time I call to him. The danger of death was
all around me; the horrors of the grave closed in on me; I was
filled with fear and anxiety. Then I called to the Lord, 'I beg you,
Lord, save me!' The Lord is merciful and good; our God is com-
passionate. The Lord protects the helpless.*

*"When I was in danger, he saved me. Be confident, my heart,
because the Lord has been good to me. The Lord saved me from
death; he stopped my tears and kept me from defeat. And so I
walk in the presence of the Lord, in the world of the living. . . ."*

From that point on Kelly clung to the words in that passage
and felt certain that she, too, would walk again in the presence of
the Lord in the world of the living.

Two months passed, and doctors performed surgery on Kelly's

neck, placing her in a halo brace and later other braces to help stabilize her broken back. During that time she continued to amaze doctors by regaining strength and movement during physical therapy sessions.

On August 21, not three months after the accident, Kelly was released from the hospital and given permission to attend high school in a wheelchair. A week later, on the first day of her senior year, using a cane and assisted by her mother, Kelly walked to the bus stop. When she arrived at school she hung her cane in a school locker and painstakingly, without any assistance, walked to her first class.

The wheelchair never made it out of the car, and on May 27, 1982, one year after the accident, Kelly donned a graduation gown and walked proudly to the Buckeye High podium to accept her diploma.

One week later, while tears filled the eyes of family and friends, Kelly walked gracefully down the aisle of their church and married her childhood sweetheart. Her doctors had told her there was no medical explanation for her recovery, and had called it miraculous.

"God was merciful and he healed me completely," Kelly said after the ceremony.

Indeed. Two years later, defying medical understanding, Kelly gave birth to the couple's first child. Today she and Ted have been married thirteen years and have three children, ages eleven, nine, and three.

"We should never, ever limit God," Kelly says now. "Ask him for help even when the situation seems hopeless. I'm living proof that he hears us and he does answer."

A Voice in the Cockpit

*D*avid Moore had never flown before, but that Sunday night in July 1971, when he was offered the opportunity to fly from Texas to North Carolina to see his wife and infant daughter, David didn't hesitate.

"What time do we leave?" he asked his friend, Henry Gardner. The man was a local crop duster and he owned a small Cessna 180. He had planned to take a sightseeing trip the next day, and was willing to go out of his way to see that David and his family were reunited. The past nine weeks had been especially traumatic for the Moore family, and Gardner wanted to do what he could to help.

The trouble began when David, twenty-four, and Florence, twenty-one, his wife, discovered that her mother was dying of cancer. The sick woman lived in Hendersonville, North Carolina—at least a two-day drive from Yoakum, Texas, where the young couple and their infant daughter lived. The situation was especially difficult because David had recently been named pastor of Hebron Baptist Church, a position which required his presence—especially on Sundays.

"We'll work out a schedule," David assured his wife, "so that we can spend as much time as possible in North Carolina."

The staff at Hebron Baptist was completely understanding, and arranged for David to take a partial leave of absence. As long as Florence's mother was ill, David could be gone during the week and then home for the Sunday morning service.

The couple decided that Florence and their daughter would stay in North Carolina while David drove the weekly commute to Texas. Nine times David made the round-trip trek before he began feeling the strain of the routine.

"I need to rest," he admitted to Florence one evening as he was preparing to return to Texas once again.

"Honey, why don't you take the bus?" She was worried about his long hours on the road. "That way you can sleep, or catch up on your plans for Sunday, and it won't be so hard on you."

David thought for a moment. "Good idea," he said, rubbing his tired eyes. "And you could have the car so you'd have some way to get around if you need to."

He boarded a passenger bus late that week determined to spend the next two days resting. Instead, the trip was a nightmarish forty-six hours of crying babies, constant stops, and loud conversations. His family was on a tight budget, and he could not afford to fly. But David was more exhausted than ever before, and he decided he'd rather walk back to North Carolina, or hitchhike the highways, than ride another bus for two straight days.

Over the weekend, Henry Gardner's daughter—a member of Hebron Baptist Church—caught wind of David's need to find a way back to North Carolina. She told her father, and on Sunday night Henry called with his offer.

"It's a small plane, but smooth as honey in the air," Henry said. "You can be my navigator."

In the recesses of his mind David felt a slight wave of anxiety course through his body. He had always been wary of small planes, and expected that when the time came for him to fly it would be on a jumbo jet. He pushed aside his momentary fears and cleared his throat.

"I've never done any navigating," he said with a laugh. "But I'd be willing to fly the plane myself if it meant getting back to my family."

David met Henry the next day at a small airport outside town. The morning was beautiful, clear, and without any trace of bad weather.

"Looks like we picked a good day to hit the skies," Henry said, easily shifting his body into the cockpit.

David sized up the tiny aircraft and silently, almost unconsciously, whispered a prayer: *Lord, guide us as we go and please get us there safely*

For the first half hour the craft flew easily through the clear skies, but as they neared Houston they entered a thick fog.

"No problem," Henry said, pointing out the windshield. "You can see the Houston radio towers there above the fog. If we keep our eyes on them we'll know where we are. Besides, we have aviation maps on board. Everything will be fine."

For a while, it looked as if Henry would be right. Then, when the plane was just outside Jackson, Mississippi, the fog worsened so that the plane became cocooned in a cloud with no visibility whatsoever.

Almost at the same time, the plane's radio and instruments died. Suddenly, the men could no longer see anything on the ground, and because of the instrument failure they couldn't monitor the fuel or talk to people in the control tower.

David may have been inexperienced at flying, but he did not need a pilot's license to know that they were in grave danger. His thoughts turned to his pretty young wife and their sixteen-month-old daughter. The couple was in the process of adopting the child, and they were expecting to sign the final papers any time. *Please,*

God, help us, he prayed silently, his hands clenched and his face white with terror. *Please, get us through this safely.*

At that moment they flew through a clearing in the fog and caught a glimpse of the small Jackson airport just below. Henry maneuvered the craft through the opening in the clouds and smoothly down onto the runway.

"Thank God," David whispered as the men climbed out of the plane and Henry began tinkering with the fuse box. A burned-out fuse had caused the instrument failure, and Henry replaced it while David telephoned Florence.

"Listen, honey," David told Florence, "we're running late because of bad weather. Meet me at the Asheville Airport about an hour later than we planned."

"Is everything okay? With the plane, I mean?" she asked. David could hear how Florence was trying to control the concern in her voice.

"It's fine," he said, sounding more confident than he felt. "I love you, honey. See you in a few hours."

As they climbed back in the craft, David again uttered a silent prayer: *You got us this far, God. Please see us through safely to North Carolina.*

In less than an hour the men were back in the sky, enjoying the fact that the sun had come out and the conditions were once again clear. By the time they flew over Atlanta, Georgia, David's fears had nearly disappeared and he began looking forward to being with his family.

Then, as the plane passed Greenville, South Carolina, the fog appeared once more, and almost instantly engulfed the small craft in a dense, suffocating blanket of gray. Moments later they approached a mountain range, and David watched as Henry struggled to clear it safely.

"After these mountains it should be sunny again," David said, struggling to convince himself as much as Henry. "There's never fog in this area."

But that afternoon there was indeed fog, and it was so thick the men could see nothing past the plane's windshield. The airport wasn't far away, and Henry immediately contacted the Asheville Airport for assistance.

"We're closed because of fog," the air traffic controller informed Henry. "We have no capability for instrument landing. Return to Greenville and land there."

"I can't," Henry said, a tinge of panic creeping into his voice. "We're almost out of fuel. We don't have enough to fly back to Greenville."

For a moment, the cockpit was eerily silent. They had no visibility, and David's eyes fell on the fuel gauge and the needle, which danced dangerously over the letter E. Again he silently prayed, struggling to control his terror: *Please, God, please get us out of these clouds safely.*

Finally, a different voice broke the silence: "Okay. We'll get the ground crew ready. Come in on an emergency landing."

David clutched the sides of his seat, his eyes wide in disbelief. There was no way they could make an emergency landing when visibility between the plane and the control tower was completely cut off by the fog.

Henry's voice snapped David to attention.

"Get the aviation maps."

David opened them instantly, and Henry estimated their location. According to the map, they should be directly above the airport. Gradually, Henry began to descend through the fog toward the ground. As he did, the voice of the controller entered the cockpit.

"Pull it up! Pull it up!"

Henry responded immediately, just as both men saw a split in the fog. They were not over the airport as they had thought. Instead they were over a busy interstate highway, and had missed an overpass bridge by no more than five feet.

David felt his heart thumping wildly, and he was struck by the certainty of one thing. Short of divine intervention, there was no way they would escape their grave situation alive.

At that instant, the controller's voice broke the silence once again. "If you will listen to me, I'll help you get down," he said.

Henry released a pent-up sigh. "Go ahead. I'm listening."

David closed his eyes momentarily and prayed, begging God to guide them safely through the fog onto the ground.

Meanwhile, the controller began guiding Henry toward a landing.

"Come down a little. Okay, a little more. Not that much. All right, now over to the right. Straighten it out and come down a little more."

The calm, reassuring voice of the controller continued its steady stream of directions, and Henry, intent on the voice, did as he was instructed. The trip seemed to take an eternity, and David wondered whether he would see his wife and daughter again. "Please, God," he whispered. "Get us onto the ground, God. Please."

The controller continued. "Raise it a little more. Okay, you're too far to the left. That's right. Now lower it a little more. All right, you're right over the end of the runway. Set it down. Now!"

Carefully responding just as he was told, Henry lowered the plane, and when he was a few feet from the ground the runway came into sight. As the plane touched down David saw Florence standing nearby waiting for him, and his eyes filled with tears of relief and gratitude.

The two men looked at each other and without saying a word, they bowed their heads and closed their eyes. "Thank you, God," David said, his voice choked with emotion. "Thank you for sparing our lives today. And thank you for listening."

Henry picked up the plane's radio and contacted the control tower.

"Hey, I just want to thank you so much for what you did. We couldn't have made it without those directions. You probably saved our lives."

There was a brief pause. "What are you talking about?" the controller asked. He had a different voice this time, and he was clearly confused. "We lost all radio contact with you when we told you to return to Greenville."

Goose bumps rose up on David's arms, and he watched as Henry's face went blank in disbelief. "You *what?*" he asked.

"We never heard from you again and we never heard you talking to us or to anyone else," the controller said. "We were stunned when we saw you break through the clouds right over the runway. It was a perfect landing."

David and Henry looked at each other in a way that needed no words. If the Asheville controller hadn't been in contact with them through the emergency landing, who had? Whose calm, clear voice had filled the cockpit with the directions that saved their lives?

Today, twenty-four years later, David is aware that he still cannot specifically answer those questions. But in his heart he is certain that Heaven heard his prayers that afternoon.

"I believe that God protected us that day and that perhaps he allowed an angel to guide us to the ground safely," David says. "God sustained me then, and he continues to do so every day of my life."

ANSWER FIFTEEN:

The Best Friend of All

*L*orri Bolton's husband needed to say just two words to turn her entire life upside down.

"We're moving!" he announced one day. Then he went on to tell her that he'd found a job in Southern California where he could concentrate on his career in solar energy.

Lorri knew this day might come. She had known it since marrying Kevin the year before. But at nineteen she wasn't ready to leave Kansas, especially with her family and friends just three short hours away.

"I can't move," she said. Tears welled up in her eyes and she hugged her body tightly. "Kevin, we've only been married a year. Can't you give it some time before we head across the country looking for work?"

Kevin's face softened. He had hoped Lorri would be excited for him, but he was sympathetic to how she felt. Her entire life had been centered around the Midwest. She was probably terrified about moving.

"Honey, you knew I wanted to work in California when you married me," he said. He stroked her cheek gently with the back of his hand. "It'll be all right. You'll stay in touch with your friends here in Kansas. You'll be able to come back and visit. Besides, you'll make new friends in no time at all."

Tears trickled down Lorri's face, and she closed her eyes. She remembered how in love she'd been with Kevin and how they had talked about moving west when he could find a job in the solar industry. He was right. Back then she *had* been supportive of his intentions.

She released a shaky sigh and nodded.

"Does that mean you're coming with me?" Kevin teased, tickling the underside of her chin and searching for a smile.

Lorri swallowed back a sob. "Of course, Kevin. I love you; you know that. I'd follow you to the moon. It's just going to be so hard."

Kevin pulled her into a hug and stroked her long hair. "I know, honey. I know."

"I can't even imagine telling them good-bye after so many years," she cried. "But at least I'll have you and the cats."

Kevin's body grew stiff and he pulled away from her.

"Now, honey, that's something we need to talk about," he said.

"What?" Lorri sniffed, wiping her cheeks with her fingertips.

"About the cats," he began. "There's no way we can bring them, honey. We're flying to California and once we get there, we'll probably rent an apartment that doesn't allow pets. We'll have to find another home for them."

"Kevin, you can't be serious?" Lorri raised her voice. She and Kevin had picked out Tigger and Tabby from an animal shelter eighteen months earlier. In that year and a half Lorri had grown very attached to them.

"Lorri, be sensible," he implored. "Can you imagine what it'd be like trying to move them into an apartment?"

For a moment Lorri considered telling him to go by himself.

It was one thing to take her away from her family and friends who were just three hours away. But if it meant leaving her cats, Lorri wasn't sure she could go.

She had married Kevin too young, at age *eighteen*, and then moved with him to Independence. The cats were the closest friends Lorri had within a three-hour radius of home.

"It won't be possible to bring them, Lorri, don't you see?" Kevin said, interrupting her silence as he tried to help her understand.

She stared at her husband, and recognized something tender and loving in his eyes. Suddenly her angry resolve dissipated. Kevin was not trying to be cruel to her by asking her to leave the cats behind. He was being sensible. He was right, and even as she felt her world crumbling around her, Lorri knew he was right. The cats would hate living in the city.

"You're right," she sobbed, burying her head in Kevin's chest and giving in to a flood of tears. "Ah, Kevin, how am I going to make it?"

"Lorri, you'll make friends easily." His voice was soothing, and she relaxed against him. "We'll both be fine. It'll be the best thing that's ever happened to us. You'll see."

But the move was even harder than Lorri anticipated. She found a good home for her cats and bade them a tearful good-bye. Then, a week later, she wore dark glasses and cried much of the time as she sorted through an entire childhood of memories and keepsakes, deciding what to bring and what to box up and take to her mother's.

Eventually the day came when she and Kevin loaded their belongings into his station wagon. They drove silently to Lorri's mother's house, where they spent the afternoon, and then set out for the airport.

"Take care of yourself," Lorri said, her voice choked so that only a squeaky whisper came out. "I love you, Mom."

Her mother nodded, too upset to speak. She simply hugged

her daughter tightly and nodded toward the car, her lower lip quivering in a way that threatened an ocean of tears.

The flight across the country was quiet and somber, with Lorri lost in thoughts of all she'd left behind. Kevin, meanwhile, was ecstatic, but he politely kept his enthusiasm to himself. He couldn't wait to leave the simpler country life behind him and begin making his mark in the world of solar energy.

When they arrived, the Boltons found a small, one-bedroom apartment not far from where Kevin would be working. Soon afterward they joined a church in the area, and Lorri decided to have a positive attitude.

But as the weeks passed she grew more homesick, constantly thinking of all she'd left behind and wishing there was some way she could turn back the clock to a time when Kevin had never heard of the job opening in California. She knew her attitude was affecting Kevin, and she was sorry. She loved him, and she wanted their time together to be fun and filled with laughter. But she couldn't seem to shake the feeling of isolation.

Two months later they purchased a beautiful home with a swimming pool, but even that didn't help. Worst of all, she felt far from God, almost as if he were unaware of her situation, unable to help her feel better.

"I'm sorry I've been so sad lately," she told Kevin one evening three months after their move to Southern California. "I don't want to spoil your excitement. I really am glad about your new job and all. It's just that sometimes I feel so lonely it's almost like I'm suffocating."

Kevin thought about Lorri's statement, and came up with what he thought might be the perfect solution. The next week, on Lorri's birthday, he presented her with a tiny black kitten.

"Oh, Kevin, he's perfect," she squealed, taking him into her arms.

For the first time since their move Lorri looked genuinely happy, and Kevin congratulated himself on finding the perfect birthday present for her.

"He'll have to be a house cat. He won't have acres of fields to play in, but he won't know any different," Kevin said. "Happy birthday, honey."

Lorri named the kitten Theo, and with a new friend to keep her company, her outlook changed overnight. She enrolled at the local university and attended morning classes. Then she would hurry home to share the afternoon with Theo.

She spent hours playing with him and training him, much as she had done with Tigger and Tabby. Sometimes when her homework was finished, she would scoop Theo into her arms and take him outside by the pool for fresh air and sunshine.

Since Theo was primarily an indoor cat, the Boltons took him to the veterinarian to be declawed. After that, they were careful not to let him jump the fence; without his claws he would have no way to defend himself.

Sometimes Lorri would lose track of Theo and the kitten would attempt to climb over the fence. But when that happened, the dogs on either side of the Boltons' home would bark ferociously, and Lorri would call Theo back into his own yard.

Theo had developed a keen ear for Lorri's voice and whenever she called him, he would meow and scamper immediately back to her side.

"That's a good boy," Lorri would say, cuddling Theo close to her and rubbing him behind his ears.

She was so thankful for Theo. When Kevin wasn't around, he was the only friend she had. She didn't know what she would have done without him. Although she still missed her family and friends back in Kansas, Lorri's days were no longer unbearably lonely.

Then one day her warning system failed. One of the neighbors had taken their dog out for a walk, and by the time Lorri realized what had happened, Theo had disappeared. Concerned, Lorri contacted both next-door neighbors and asked them to search their yards for the black kitten. When neither found Theo, Lorri told herself that he would return within a few hours when he got hungry.

lock came, and then six. Still Theo had not returned,
as beginning to panic. Kevin arrived home, and they
surrounding streets.

Theo, here kitty, kitty, kitty," Lorri called as they walked.
They searched for two hours, but there was no sign of the kitten.

Two days passed. Each afternoon Lorri rushed home from her
classes hoping to find her kitten home where he belonged. She
walked up and down her neighborhood each afternoon asking
neighbors if they'd seen her black kitten and calling Theo's name.

By the third afternoon, Lorri began to lose hope. She walked
home thinking she would probably never see the cat again. If Theo
hadn't come home by then, something must have happened to him.
Perhaps he had been picked up by someone and taken home.

She set her books on the kitchen counter and went into the
backyard.

"Theo," she called as loud as she could. "Here, Theo."

She stood waiting for a response, until finally the fear and
loneliness she felt became overwhelming and she turned back toward the house, running into her bedroom.

There, she threw herself on her bed and began yelling at God.
She thought of a Bible verse in Lamentations that says, "Pour out
your heart like water in the presence of the Lord."

That was exactly what she did.

"Lord, I can't handle this! I'm so lonely and Theo was all I
had. Now he's gone, too," she sobbed loudly. "I just can't handle
this, Lord. It's too much."

She continued for several minutes until her anger and frustration were spent. Then, still crying, she remembered another scripture, Psalms 34:18, which says, "The Lord is close to the
brokenhearted and saves those who are crushed in spirit."

Suddenly, Lorri felt God's presence, and in her grief she clung
to the feeling. The chasm that had developed between her and God
disappeared in an instant, and she felt as if she'd found a long-lost
friend.

No longer angry, she looked upward and whispered yet another prayer. "Please, Lord, hear me now. I need my cat to come home." She thought a moment. "I'm going to go out into the back-yard and I need for you to bring Theo home for me. If it is your will, Lord, please answer my prayer."

Lorri realized that her request sounded childish, but she trusted with all her heart that God could hear her. She walked down the hallway and opened the back door.

There, sitting by the pool, was Theo. He glanced at her casu-ally as if he'd been there all the time.

"Meow," he squeaked, scampering toward her.

Lorri fell to her knees, bowing her head in thanks. Not just because her cat was back home. But because she had rediscovered the best friend of all.

The Call of Reassurance

*F*or the last twelve years of her life, Alverna Kirsch-enman shared an extremely close relationship with her daughter, Twyla Ward. In 1980, Alverna was diagnosed with scleroderma and polymyositis—degenerative muscle and connective-tissue disorders that cause a gradual wasting of the body and eventually result in death. Alverna was just forty-six when she learned of the diagnosis, and she shared the news with her three grown children immediately, asking them to pray for her.

"None of us really knows how long we've got," she told them. "But please pray for me all the same. Pray that I don't leave any of you until God himself is ready to take me."

As the years passed, Alverna's condition worsened. She lost the use of her arms and legs, and eventually was confined to a wheelchair. During that time, Twyla's brother and sister moved away from Sioux Falls, South

Dakota, to start their own families. Twyla and her husband, Tony, stayed behind to care for Alverna.

"I don't know what I'd do without you, Twyla," her mother told her on several occasions. "You are more than I ever could have hoped for in a daughter."

Alverna spent much of her time at the home of Twyla and Tony. When the couple's children were born—first Karly, then Haley—Alverna thrived on watching them grow.

Although she couldn't do the more physical things she'd hoped to do as a grandmother, she could tell them stories and listen to them when they played make-believe. The relationship between Alverna and Twyla's family grew, and Twyla could sense that her children had a special understanding of their grandmother's poor health.

By the beginning of 1992, Alverna was fifty-eight, and completely crippled by her diseases. There were heartbreaking times when Twyla would spend an afternoon with her mother and the children, only to watch Alverna grow weary and be forced to take a nap. Twyla would watch her mother sleeping and wonder how she was going to deal with the woman's inevitable death. Alverna's muscles and connective tissues were almost completely destroyed, and now the crippling disease had settled in her lungs, making it hard for her to breathe. The doctors had warned that she might not live through the year.

Summer came, and Alverna struggled, managing to survive through the autumn. Then, almost overnight, her condition worsened dramatically and she had to be hospitalized because of the congestion in her lungs. Twyla kept a vigil at her mother's bedside, praying for her and singing familiar, comforting songs. Although the entire body is affected by scleroderma and polymyositis, it does not affect the mind. For that reason, Twyla felt it was especially important to stay by her mother's side in her final days.

"Thank you, Twyla," Alverna said one morning, wrestling with each word. "It means so much that you are here."

Each day Alverna's health deteriorated more. Soon she could

barely talk, but many times she would look at Twyla in such a way that Twyla was sure her mother was listening to her, thankful for her daughter's prayers and songs. The days passed, and Twyla remained determined to stay by her mother's side until there was no longer a reason to be there.

On the day before Thanksgiving, November 25, 1992, Alverna seemed worse than at any time before. Twyla sat beside her, tears streaming down her face as she held her mother's hand tightly in her own.

"I love you, Mom," she said, bending over and looking into her mother's eyes. Alverna blinked, her crippled body motionless, her breathing labored.

"Mom," Twyla continued, "I know you can hear me, so listen to what I have to say. You've been such a wonderful mother, so good with my children. I want you to know how much we all love you, Mom. And I want you to know that we'll all be together again some day. I promise."

Alverna remained still, but her eyes filled with tears.

Looking up toward heaven, Twyla began to pray. "Dear God our father, please be kind with my mother. Please help her reach your light and give her peace as she goes. Thank you for her love, Lord. Help us find a way to survive without her."

Once more Twyla's eyes searched those of her mother's, and this time Twyla felt as if her mother was trying to smile. Then, very peacefully, Alverna slipped into a coma.

For the next few hours, although she was unconscious, Alverna's mouth made subtle movements as if she was talking to someone. Twyla continued holding her hand, singing and praying for her.

"It's all right, Mom," Twyla said quietly, her voice calm despite the tears that still trickled down her cheeks. "Go to the light, Mom. The Lord is ready for you now."

Twyla mentioned the names of her mother's parents and of her son, who had died when he was just two.

"They're waiting for you, Mom," Twyla continued. "They're all waiting. It's all right. Let go and go to the light."

Finally, at 12:15 a.m. on Thanksgiving Day, Alverna died.

At the exact moment, Twyla sat up straighter in her chair, certain that the body before her no longer housed her mother's spirit. A tremendous peace, like something she'd never known before in her life, came over her and she smiled through her tears.

"You're there, aren't you, Mom?" she asked. "You're home." Then she smiled. Life would be hard without Alverna, but the indescribable peace that filled Twyla's heart was like an assurance that things had worked out for the best. Everything was going to be okay.

That week was hectic as Twyla's brother and sister arrived from different parts of the country to aid in planning their mother's funeral. Together they went through their mother's small house and made decisions about her belongings.

The whirlwind of activity quieted down almost immediately after the funeral, when the rest of the family was forced to return to their homes to get back to work. Since Twyla lived so close to her mother's house, she had agreed to take care of all the remaining business involving Alverna's death. Meanwhile she continued to work as a designer at a local florist shop and take care of Karly, seven, and Haley, four.

Before long, the peace that had helped her through the initial days after her mother's death had all but disappeared. Instead, Twyla felt desperately lonely and overwhelmed with the idea of selling her mother's house and with the amount of work left to do.

One night after Tony was asleep, she buried her head in her pillow and sobbed. Silently, drowning in the pain of losing her mother, she began to pray.

"Sweet Lord, please help me to feel that peace that I felt at first. I believe Mom is with you now, but help me to really know it in my heart. Help me feel your peace once again. And let me know everything's going to be okay."

The next day Twyla was up early as usual, preparing the children's lunches, when the phone rang. Tony had already been gone more than an hour, and she wondered as she reached for the cordless receiver whether he might be calling. Just before she picked it up, she realized that the phone in the next room was not ringing. Sound came only from the cordless phone in the kitchen.

"Hello?" Her voice sounded tired, and despair from the night before still hung over her like a cloud.

When no one responded, Twyla tried again. "Hello? Is anyone there?"

Still there was only silence. Twyla shrugged and hung up the phone.

An hour later, when Karly was off to school and Twyla and Haley were reading a book on the sofa, the phone rang again. As before, only the cordless phone was ringing. Twyla set down the storybook and walked into the kitchen for the phone.

"Hello?" she said.

Silence.

"Is there someone there?" Twyla asked. "Say something if you're there."

But there was no sound at all from the other end. Shrugging once more, Twyla hung up the phone and returned to the sofa where Haley was waiting for her.

Nearly two hours later Twyla was making lunch for Haley when once again only the cordless phone rang. This time Twyla sighed loudly in frustration as she reached for the receiver.

"Hello?" Her tone had grown aggravated; she had nearly run out of patience. She had much to get done that day and didn't have time for prank callers.

When no one responded, Twyla wasted no time. She pushed the disconnect button, waited for a dial tone, and immediately dialed the number of her friend Jim.

"Jim'll know what to do about this," she muttered.

When he answered, she told him what had happened.

"The strange thing is it's only ringing on my cordless phone," she told Jim. "The other phone isn't making any noise at all."

Jim suggested she unplug the phone from the electrical outlet.

"Might be a malfunction. But it can't ring if it isn't getting any electricity," Jim said. "That should solve the problem for now, but you might want to have that phone looked at when you get a chance."

Twyla thanked him for his suggestion, and immediately unplugged the cordless phone.

"That solves that problem," she said out loud.

Thirty minutes later, the phone rang again and Twyla wrinkled her brow curiously. Once again, only the cordless phone was ringing, but it seemed impossible since there was no electricity feeding the phone's base unit.

"Hello?" she said. "Is anyone there?"

When no one answered, Twyla hung up and phoned Jim once more.

"Unplug it from the phone jack," Jim advised. "That way it won't be hooked up to anything at all. No way for it to ring after that."

Twyla hung up and followed Jim's instructions. She even pulled the phone away from the wall and bundled up the detached cording. Mentally she made a note to take the unit in for repair.

Haley was down for a nap, and another hour passed as Twyla sifted through paperwork regarding her mother's death.

"This is hard, Lord," she sighed, feeling tears once again gathering in her eyes. "I miss her so badly."

Suddenly the early afternoon silence was broken by the ringing of the telephone. Twyla walked into the bedroom and saw that the wall phone was not ringing. She followed the sound and felt a chill run through her body.

The cordless phone—no longer attached to either the electrical outlet or the phone jack—was ringing. Overcome by a combination of fear and curiosity, Twyla moved slowly toward the phone and gingerly picked up the receiver.

"Hello?" Twyla's voice was soft, uncertain. Once again there was only silence at the other end.

Suddenly Twyla remembered the date. It was December 11, her mother's birthday. In the sea of responsibilities and duties she had forgotten what day it was.

Instantly she was flooded by the same feeling of peace that had washed over her the moment her mother had died. She thought about the prayer she had said the night before, and knew in that moment that God had answered her.

She had called to him for help and now he was calling her. Just to let her know she was loved and that everything really was going to be okay.

ANSWER SEVENTEEN:

Heaven's Perfect Timing

*J*amie Baron did so much commuting that she had become an expert at deciphering the road conditions and weather patterns in Western Pennsylvania. But the winter of 1993-94 was the coldest and fiercest in a hundred years, and even Jamie had a deep respect for the types of storms that might blow in with little notice. The roads were perilous because of the weather, and everyday people were killed on the highways and rural roads because of the severe driving conditions.

That winter Jamie, twenty-nine, could be found in any of half-a-dozen places within a hundred-mile radius. She lived in Boswell, Pennsylvania; worked days in Somerset as the director of social services for a community organization; taught college courses some evenings in Cresson; and on the remaining nights took graduate courses in Indiana, Pennsylvania. In her remaining spare time she sometimes did her shopping in Altoona.

Her commute between locations often took more than an hour one way, so that winter as a precaution she turned in her old four-door and purchased a brand-new Ford Tempo.

"At least now I won't have to worry about breaking down in a storm," Jamie told her fiancé, Tim.

Tim, thirty-eight, worked days at Tableland Social Services with Jamie, and was worried about the amount of time she spent commuting between school, both jobs, and home. He was relieved that she had decided to purchase a new car.

"You still have to be careful," Tim advised her one afternoon as the couple ate lunch together at the Wendy's fast-food restaurant in Somerset. "You know how the storms can be. They can come from out of nowhere."

"You're right, but don't worry," Jamie assured him. "I'll be careful. Besides, I have my cellular phone if anything goes wrong."

One of the pleasures of their busy lives was the time they took each day to share lunch at the local Wendy's near the social services office where they worked. That day was particularly cold, and Jamie and Tim savored the warmth of the restaurant and their brief time together.

"Any plans for this afternoon?" Tim picked up an onion ring and slipped it into his mouth.

"Need you ask?" Jamie teased. "Actually, I have the afternoon off and I don't teach tonight. Graduate class isn't until seven o'clock, so I thought I'd check out the furniture stores in Altoona between now and then."

For weeks Jamie had been purchasing items to furnish her newly remodeled office in Somerset. She still hadn't found a curio cabinet, and figured she'd have several stores to choose from if she could spend a few hours searching in Altoona.

Tim's face fell at the mention of the larger town. "That means you have to cross the Summit," he said. "You know how danger-ous that can be, Jamie."

Jamie nervously fiddled with her cheeseburger and gazed out-side. "I know, but look at the sky. The news said there's no snow in sight until tomorrow. I need to go sometime, and there couldn't be a better day to drive the Summit, don't you think?"

Tim shrugged. "It's clear and calm now, but keep an eye on it," he said. "Please."

Jamie took his hand in hers and smiled. "Don't worry. I won't take any chances."

Three hours later Jamie walked out of the fourth Altoona furniture store of the afternoon, and was surprised to see menacing clouds moving in over the city. She remembered Tim's warning and looked at her watch. It was nearly four, and it would take ninety minutes to reach the university in Indiana.

Even though she hadn't found the perfect cabinet for her office, she decided she'd better begin her long drive. It would be better to cross the Summit now and have time to spare in Indiana than to wait and have a storm blow in. Jamie looked skyward again, and noticed that the air had grown very still. She shuddered. Her life had been filled with enough severe snowstorms to understand what the stillness meant. The storm was ready to bear down on anything in its path. She reached into her purse for her car keys, and ran lightly across the parking lot toward her car.

"Please, God," she whispered aloud, "let me get through safely. Don't let me cross that Summit if it's going to be too dangerous."

As she drove along surface streets toward the on-ramp of Route 22, she considered the frightening Summit and again prayed for safety. What if the storm hit before she had time to cross? She would have to drive up the steep grade of the Allegheny Mountains before reaching the Summit, where the roadway leveled out at the top of the mountain range. Route 22 was extremely dangerous there because, without the protection of surrounding mountains, crosswinds made driving treacherous even in mild weather. Signs warning drivers about the danger of crosswinds were scattered along the Summit. Nevertheless, accidents were commonplace.

Jamie continued making her way toward the on-ramp, frustrated by the heavy traffic. There seemed to be a sense of panic and confusion among the other drivers as people flooded the roads attempting to reach their destinations before the storm hit. Wind began blowing, and Jamie was thankful that Route 22 was less than a block away.

Then, up ahead, she spotted a Wendy's restaurant.

Suddenly she felt a strong urge to pull in and order something from the drive-through window. Jamie shook off the feeling, determined to stay on the road since every minute might be crucial in clearing the Summit before the storm. The traffic crept forward, and again Jamie was nearly overcome with the desire to pull off the road and get something to eat.

"This is crazy," she muttered. "I never eat before class and I never eat fast food for dinner."

She reasoned with herself that she had finished a large meal less than four hours earlier and had no time to stop for food with the storm looming ahead. She was determined to wait until she arrived at the university campus before eating, but still the unaccountable urge persisted. As she drew closer to the Wendy's, her skin became hot and tingly and she felt light-headed. Jamie recognized that the feelings could be symptoms of low blood sugar. Just as she was about to pass the restaurant and proceed down the road, she heard a voice clearly instructing her to stop and eat.

At the last possible instant, Jamie stepped on the brake and turned into the Wendy's parking lot toward the drive-through window.

Still baffled by the voice and her own actions, Jamie ordered a cheeseburger, and then waited anxiously while the cashier seemed to take an eternity preparing and bagging her order.

"Come on," Jamie muttered under her breath as she paid for her food. The sky was growing still darker, and she was terrified at what would happen if she didn't get on the highway soon.

The cashier handed her the burger and Jamie drove off. She was about to pull back into traffic when another wave of heat and clamminess washed over her. The feeling was similar to that of being faint, but there was something different about it. Almost as if the heat was emanating from somewhere inside her body. She saw an open parking spot and without thinking, she pulled her Ford Tempo into the spot and turned off the engine.

"Why am I wasting so much time?" she asked, angry with herself. "I've got to get on the road."

She loosened her coat and seat belt and quickly ate the cheeseburger. Instantly she felt better, and in a moment the intense heat and clammy feeling were gone completely. There had been times when Jamie had felt light-headed and needed energy, but never had eating caused them to disappear so quickly.

Her strength renewed, Jamie strapped her seat belt back into place and eased her car into traffic. Although the sky was frighteningly dark, there was still no snow, and she whispered a prayer of thanks as she drove up the on-ramp for Route 22 and began climbing toward the Summit.

Minutes later, as she continued to climb, snowflakes began to fall on her windshield. She drew a deep breath, preparing herself for the treacherous conditions that might lay ahead, then turned on her headlights. Careful to leave a safe distance between her car and the one in front of her, Jamie continued up the mountain.

As she drew closer to the Summit, the snow began coming down in sheets.

"Dear God, please guide me, please help me to drive safely," she prayed aloud.

Gripping the steering wheel tightly with both hands, Jamie continued to fear the worst as the highway began to level into the Summit. Suddenly, without the protection of the mountain range, the snow completely engulfed the roadway in a matter of seconds. Jamie was in the middle of a whiteout, with wind howling in different directions and huge snowflakes making it impossible to see more than a few feet.

Jamie's heart beat wildly as she gently pumped the brake, aware that if someone hit her from behind even a minor accident could send her through the guardrails, tumbling to certain death thousands of feet below. She fixed her eyes ahead, glancing occasionally into the rearview mirror.

One minute passed, then two. Finally Jamie saw that the car she was following had stopped. She could see only his taillights immediately in front of her, and had no idea whether either car was still on the highway. But at least she was no longer moving through the blinding snow, and when she saw lights stopping behind her as well she allowed herself to feel relieved. *The traffic's stopped everywhere,* she thought. *Now we'll just have to wait it out.*

Minutes passed and then abruptly, as quickly as it had settled over them, the snow cloud lifted and Jamie could see that she was the tenth car behind a jackknifed tractor-trailer blocking the road.

"Thank God," Jamie murmured, noting that there appeared to be no injuries and that the tractor-trailer seemed to have suffered only minor damage. Jamie picked up her cellular phone and dialed her professor's office number.

"It's Jamie Baron; I won't be at class tonight," Jamie stated when the professor answered the phone. "I'm stuck up here on the Summit."

The professor offered her sympathy and gave Jamie the following week's assignment.

"Listen, I'm sorry you can't make it, but don't kill yourself trying to get home," the professor said. "The weather is atrocious and I'm worried about the other students commuting over the Summit."

The traffic began to inch forward. "I know," Jamie replied. "The roads everywhere must be a mess in this storm."

As the traffic continued to inch past the tractor-trailer Jamie suddenly shrieked.

"What?" the professor asked, her voice filled with alarm. "Jamie, are you there?"

"You can't believe what I'm seeing," Jamie said.

On the other side of the jackknifed truck there were dozens of cars smashed together, piled on top of each other in the ditch between the two sides of the highway. It was easy to see what had happened. When the whiteout had come upon the Summit, the drivers had done everything possible to avoid going over the cliffs. In doing so they had overcompensated and driven into the center ditch, hitting each other head-on in several cases.

Jamie explained the scene to her professor.

"You better go," the professor warned. "Be careful."

Jamie hung up and stopped her car. The man in the car in front of her did the same and climbed out, running toward the mangled stretch of vehicles. Moments later he returned and asked Jamie if he could use her cellular phone.

"It's unbelievable," he said. "There are people lying all over the road. Some of them look like they're dead." The man shook his head, and Jamie could see he was shivering. "A few minutes earlier and we'd have been in that disaster. It makes you wonder, doesn't it?"

A sudden chill went through Jamie's body, sending goose bumps along her arms and legs. She glanced at her floorboard, where the empty cheeseburger wrapper lay crumpled in a ball, and she understood the voice that had commanded her to stop. The detour had taken just seven minutes, but had probably saved her life.

Jamie handed the man her telephone and bowed her head, thanking God for sparing her from what would have been a tragic accident.

In minutes, ambulances arrived at the scene, and police ordered Jamie and the other unharmed drivers in the area to remain in their cars as rescue vehicles raced to the accident victims. An hour later they were given permission to turn around and follow a police escort back down the highway since the road was closed to all oncoming traffic.

It took nearly three hours for Jamie to drive home using a detour route, and she used that time to ponder the importance of prayer and the mercy of God. She also prayed for the victims who had not been spared. It was hard to imagine that God had been so merciful to her and yet had allowed many of the others to perish. But she knew that was part of the mystery of God. He saw things differently, and Jamie believed that only he knew the reasons things happen the way they do.

Later, a white cross was erected at the site of that afternoon's horrific pile-up on Route 22. Thirty vehicles had been involved in the accident, and nearly a dozen people had lost their lives. Yet another sign warning of the perilously dangerous crosswinds that plague the Summit and the risk of sudden storms in the area is planted near the cross.

Jamie is married now and still working two jobs, which leaves her little choice but to commute across the Summit on a regular basis. But not once since that winter afternoon has she driven that stretch of highway without first thanking and praying to her Savior.

Across the Miles

*C*harles Herch had two brothers, but he never knew either of them. The first died at birth. And the second died tragically at age four. Although he grew up something of an only child, Charles never forgot how much his parents had lost.

"Don't worry, Mom," he'd tell her when he was a young teenager. "You'll always have me around. I'm never going anywhere."

Charles's mother, Katie, would grin sadly at her son and tousle his golden-brown hair.

"The good Lord has taken two of my boys home to be with him," she'd say. "But he knows how much a person can handle, Charles. You're the boy he left for me and your father."

But when Charles turned eighteen, he was sent overseas to serve in the Korean War. The idea of losing Charles on a battlefield thousands of miles from home terrified his parents, but they prayed constantly for their son and believed God would protect him.

"Please, God, let us know when he needs our prayers," Katie would pray each night. "And bring Charles home safely to us. He's all we have left, Lord."

A year passed, during which Charles wrote to his parents as often as he could. He told them of the loss of life and the dangers he faced each day. And he asked them to keep praying for his safety.

Then on July 28, 1953, Charles was working with other infantrymen from the 2nd Infantry Division near a hill known as Outpost Harry. Charles had suffered minor injuries two days earlier, and was attempting only light duty until he was completely recovered.

It was midday, and Charles sat down for a rest some twenty feet from a supply center where the ammunition from their outpost was stored. There were grenades, shells, and other explosives.

"Hey, you're slacking off again, Herch," Ralph Dunn called out, grinning. He and a few of Charles's closest friends were standing near the ammunition taking a break. They knew that Charles had been injured, but they always enjoyed teasing each other.

"No more than you do every day of the week, Dunn," Charles retorted quickly, laughing at his buddies.

At that instant there was a terrifying explosion. Something had ignited one of the pieces of ammunition, and the entire supply area disintegrated into a ball of fire.

Ralph and four young infantrymen standing near him were killed instantly. Ten others, including Charles, were critically wounded. Bodies lay about the ground, and Charles groaned as he tried to feel where he was injured. He felt a gaping hole on his right side, and also along his neck and face. Despite the smoke and fire nearby, he was unable to move.

"Help me," he called out, his voice weak and raspy. "I'm dying over here. Someone help me."

Another soldier from his division heard him, and saw that he was bleeding badly from his injuries. He called for help, and another man joined him. Together they slid Charles onto a stretcher and ran him into an open field.

"Wait here, man," one of them shouted above the roar of confusion. "Someone'll be here soon."

Then Charles was alone. He drifted in and out of consciousness, and realized that he was bleeding to death.

"God, please don't let me die here," he whispered. "My folks need me, God."

At the same exact moment, across the world in Hamtramck, Michigan, Katie Herch sat up straight in bed screaming.

"Charlie, wake up!" Her voice was frantic and her husband shot up in bed, his eyes wide and disoriented.

"What is it, Katie?" he asked breathlessly.

"It's Charles. He's hurt; I have the feeling he needs our help."

Charlie Herch sighed and relaxed somewhat. "Katie, he's in Korea. There's no way you could know whether he was in trouble or not."

Katie nodded emphatically. "Yes, Charlie, I prayed that God would let me know when he needed our help."

Charlie frowned. "What can we do, dear, even if he *is* in trouble?"

Katie's voice returned to normal and she sat up even straighter. "We can pray for him."

Charlie nodded and took his wife's hands in his. "Okay, let's pray."

Katie bowed her head and closed her eyes as she began to pray out loud. "Lord, you've woken me from a sound sleep. I just know it's because Charles is in trouble somewhere. I don't know what he needs or where he is, Lord, but you do. Please help him, God. Whatever he needs, please provide it. In your holy name, amen."

Back in Korea, at that same instant, Charles heard a distinct voice speaking very near his ear.

"Don't worry. You are not going to die today. This is not the time or way for you."

Charles looked around, but he was completely alone in the field. The realization sent chills down his arms and he knew that the words were true, whoever had spoken them. He felt himself relax, and in a matter of minutes a helicopter landed, whisking him off to a local military hospital.

Not until two days later did Katie learn what had happened to her son. An officer came to their door and told them that Charles had been injured but was recovering.

"When was he hurt, sir?" Katie asked, feeling the hair on her arms begin to rise.

The officer looked at his information sheet. "It says here he went down July 28, sometime around two o'clock in the afternoon."

Katie quickly figured out the time difference, and realized that what she suspected had been true. God had indeed heard her prayers and directed her to pray for Charles at the exact moment of his need.

I'll Go in His Place

*I*n the summer of 1979, John Christensen was working in the yard of his home in Marion, Kansas, when he received a call from his brother's wife. He walked into the house, wiped the sweat from his brow, and picked the receiver up off the countertop.

"John, you better get down here quickly," Jim's wife blurted out. She'd been crying, and John could tell she was distraught.

"Judy, don't tell me Jim's worse?"

"Yes." She began to cry, and John's heart went out to her. "The infection's all through his body. Doctors say it doesn't look good. Please, John, hurry."

John hung up the phone and moved toward his wife, Diana, who had joined him from the next room when she realized the call was about Jim.

"I can't believe it," John said. "That was Judy. She said Jim's gotten worse and the doctors think we should all be down there."

"You mean he might not make it?" Diana was astonished.

"I guess not. We better get down there and see what's happening."

John grabbed his car keys, stunned at the turn of events. His brother, Jim, was only thirty-seven, and had been healthy and strong until the previous week, when he'd been hospitalized with appendicitis. Doctors had removed the appendix, but during the procedure the organ had burst, spewing poisonous infection throughout his body.

At first antibiotics seemed to handle the invasion of infection throughout his system. But the day before, Jim's fever had begun to rise and the family had again grown concerned. Still, even the doctors hadn't thought Jim's illness could be life-threatening until now.

John thought about what would happen if his older brother died, and he shuddered. Jim was in the prime of his life, and he and Judy had two young children. Silently he prayed that God would spare Jim and give his body strength to fight the infection.

John and Diana drove the five miles to the hospital, where they met up with John's parents.

"Is it really as bad as Judy said?" John searched his father's eyes for an answer.

"It's serious, son. Very serious. We all need to pray for him."

The sudden change in Jim's condition had caught Lynn Christensen by surprise also. He and his oldest son worked together in a family-run farm-equipment business. He saw Jim nearly every day, and knew him to be strong and in good health.

"If anyone can pull through this thing, Jim will," the older man continued. "But let's pray all the same."

John nodded and turned to hug his mother, Wilma. He saw that she had tears in her eyes, and he squeezed her hands in his.

"He's going to be all right, Mom," John assured her. "God won't let anything happen to him. Not with those little kids waiting for him back at home."

Wilma nodded, but she knew that wasn't always true. Sometimes people died and there wasn't any earthly explanation for their death. Bad things happened in life. Even to praying people. Wilma believed there was a reason behind such occurrences, but usually that reason remained a mystery. And the knowledge of that never made the tragedy easier to accept.

"Let's ask God to be merciful," she suggested softly.

The foursome moved quietly down the sterile corridors of the hospital to the intensive-care waiting room. For the next few hours there was little conversation as they passed the time praying and waiting for word from the doctors.

At about five o'clock that evening the primary doctor responsible for treating Jim entered the room. By then Jim's sister and her family had joined the others, and the waiting room was full of people worried about Jim.

"I'm afraid I don't have very good news," the doctor said softly, tucking his hands into his white medical jacket. "Jim's fever is very, very high and the blood tests show he's no longer responding to the antibiotics."

All of them knew Jim had taken a turn for the worse, so the doctor's words came as no surprise to Lynn. But still, he was puzzled over what was happening.

"Doctor, these complications are all a result of my son's appendicitis?" Lynn asked.

The doctor shook his head pensively and pursed his lips. "No, not exactly. The appendix became inflamed and caused the initial problem. Then when it burst during surgery, the infection inside spread through Jim's bloodstream, sending his entire body into immediate trauma."

He paused a moment, searching for the easiest terms to explain the situation. "Because of that, he's now fighting against peritonitis, infection throughout his body. When that happens the situation is very serious, and the outcome depends on how easily the person's immune system can handle the invading infection.

"In Jim's case, his body attempted to fight the problem, and then for some reason it shut down. At this point the infection is out of control, and there's nothing else we can do for him except continue to administer massive antibiotics."

"Doctor, when you say nothing else we can do for him, does that mean he might die?" Wilma sounded brave as she asked the question, but the others knew she was on the verge of breaking down.

"Yes, I'm afraid so. If something doesn't change, I don't think he'll make it through the night."

Diana muffled a gasp, while Judy hung her head and sighed. Lynn cleared his throat, his chin quivering with emotion. "When can we see him, sir?"

"Immediate family may take turns seeing him. Just one at a time, though," he said. Then he paused uncomfortably. This part of his job never got easier. "I'm sorry about all this. Let's hope for a miracle."

Then he turned and left the Christensen family alone to deal with the blow. Judy stood up, tears flooding her eyes, and headed toward the door.

"I'll go see him first," she said. "I'll tell him you're all here. Maybe it'll help."

Judy was prepared for what she saw when she entered her husband's room, but it was still painfully difficult. Jim was hooked up to IV tubing and his body was red with the heat of his fever. His eyes were closed and he appeared to be caught up in a fitful sleep. Could this be the same man who was the picture of health only two weeks ago?

"Honey, it's me," she whispered, leaning over his bed.

Jim moaned, and Judy was fairly sure he couldn't understand her. His fever was so high he had become delirious, and Judy took his hand, cringing at how hot it felt in her own.

"Listen, now, Jim," she said, her voice cracking with emotion. "Everyone's here; they're out in the lobby. And they're praying for you, Jim. We all want you to hurry up and fight this thing so you can come home. You hear me, honey?"

There was no response, and a single sob escaped from Judy's throat.

"Jim, please don't die. We need you. Hang in there, sweetheart." She ran her fingers tenderly over his blazing hot forehead as her tears fell on his hospital bed. "I love you, Jim."

When Judy returned, Lynn took a turn, and then Wilma, and when they had both come back to the waiting room, Diana and John exchanged a glance.

"You go," John said. "I'll go next."

It was after eight in the evening by then and the hospital had grown quiet. Diana left the room and disappeared down the hallway. The others were quiet, lost in their own thoughts and sadness.

A few minutes passed, and the silence in the room was interrupted as a heavyset, elderly woman leaned into the room. Immediately Lynn and Wilma recognized her as one of their longtime neighbors, Thelma Robinson. She was in her late seventies, a devoutly faithful woman who spent most of her days volunteering at church. Despite the walker she needed to get around, she was healthy and still spent an hour each day working in her flower garden.

"Well, I'll be," she said cheerfully. "What are you good folks doing hanging around a hospital on a nice summer night like this?"

Lynn nodded toward Thelma politely and ignored her question. "Evening, Thelma. I didn't know you were ill. You been in the hospital long?"

"Naaa," Thelma said. "Just here for a few routine tests. You know those doctors, poking and prodding and taking pictures just to tell you everything's fine." She glanced at the clock on the wall. "Well, it's about bedtime so I better get going. Just thought I'd take a stroll through the place and see if anything exciting was going on."

She looked at the many faces of the Christensen family as they sat solemnly in the waiting room, and suddenly her face fell with concern.

"Lynn, is everything okay? You people look mighty upset."

Lynn hung his head, afraid he might cry, and Wilma answered for him.

"Yes, Thelma, it's serious. It's our son, Jim, the oldest. He has peritonitis, infection all through his body." She reached for her husband's hand. "The doctors told us he probably won't live through the night."

Thelma looked appalled. "Well, now that's just not right. Jim's a young thing, isn't he? Thirty-something?"

"Thirty-seven," Wilma said softly. "His children are very young."

"Thirty-seven!" Thelma repeated, shaking her head. "And little kids, too." The older woman shifted positions, pulling her robe more closely around her body. "Well, I believe I'm going to have a talk tonight with the man upstairs and ask him to let me go in Jim's place."

The Christensen family looked at her in unison, startled by her statement. "Now, Thelma, that's not necessary," Lynn said quickly. "We're praying for Jim and we'll pray for you, too, so that . . ."

Thelma waved a hand, interrupting Lynn. "No, no. Don't go doing that. I don't need no one praying for me no more." She smiled peacefully. "Lynn, I'm more than ready to go home. I've loved our dear Lord all my life, and I'm getting too tired to stay around here anymore. I want to go home soon and it might as well be tonight."

She thought a moment before continuing.

"Here's what I'm going to do. Tonight I'm going to ask God to be kind and generous with me. I'll ask him to take me in Jim's place so that come tomorrow morning Jim'll be on the road to recovery and I'll be on the road to the Pearly Gates. Wouldn't that just be the best thing yet?"

Lynn was silent a moment, unsure of how to react.

"Well, that's all settled," Thelma said, sounding very sure of herself. "Everything will be just fine for the both of us." She smiled at Lynn and Wilma and then at the others.

"I'll see you on the other side," she said, winkin̬
she shuffled away.

Diana returned from Jim's room just as Thelma
"Wasn't that your old neighbor?" she asked Lynn aɾ
she sat down.

"Yes," Wilma said, still perplexed by Thelma's unusual words.
"She said the strangest thing. She said she was going to pray that
God takes her home tonight in Jim's place. She said she was tired
of living, she'd lived long enough, and she was ready to join God
in Heaven."

Diana raised an eyebrow and looked at the others in the room.
"She said that?"

"Now don't go putting any truth into her words," one of them
said in response. "God doesn't work like that, taking one life in
place of another."

Lynn had been very quiet, staring intently at his hands. Now
he looked up and spoke. "You never know about God," he said.
"He works in mysterious ways. Scripture says the prayer of a righteous person is powerful and effective. And I don't know many
people as righteous, really righteous in the way God intended, as
Thelma Robinson."

There was silence again, and John privately pondered the
woman's faith and her lack of fear regarding death. He didn't expect anything to come of her strange proclamation, but he felt
Thelma's words revealed a great deal of wisdom. The thought of
going to Heaven was one of pure joy for Thelma Robinson, not
sadness or sorrow. For people as close to God as she was, death
was merely a journey to the other side. John felt filled with peace,
and decided that the woman had in some ways made facing Jim's
impending death easier.

Before midnight, John and Diana and several of the others
returned home for a few hours' sleep.

"We'll be back before sunup," John said, bending to kiss his
mother on the cheek. "Call us if anything changes."

Wilma nodded. She and Lynn intended to stretch out on the

waiting room sofas. They wanted to be nearby if Jim needed them for any reason.

Three hours passed, and Lynn and Wilma drifted in and out of sleep. Several times during the night they checked on Jim, but his condition remained critical. Then at six the next morning John and Diana returned to the waiting room and nudged John's parents awake.

"How is he?" John asked.

"We haven't heard anything since a few hours ago," Lynn said, sitting up and rubbing his eyes. "He must still be hanging in there."

John and Diana sat down and held hands, bracing themselves for whatever sorrow the day might hold. They stayed that way for the next hour while other family members arrived.

Then, just before eight o'clock, Jim's doctor burst through the door, a broad smile on his face.

"His fever broke," the doctor announced. "It seems that sometime in the last couple of hours he began making a turn-around and now his fever is almost down to normal. I have no way of explaining what happened—I've never seen anything like it before."

Tears of relief flooded the family's eyes. Lynn rose from the couch and shook the doctor's hand. "Thank you, sir," he said. "Does that mean he's going to pull through this?"

"He's a new man today, Mr. Christensen. I think he's going to be just fine."

The doctor left, and the Christensens leaned back in their seats, thankful and relieved.

"Thank God," Wilma said. "Thank God for hearing our prayers."

At the mention of prayer several of them remembered Thelma Robinson and sat straighter in their chairs. They exchanged glances.

"Dad," John said, his eyes wider than before, "you don't think this has something to do with what Mrs. Robinson said last night, do you?"

"Of course not, son," Lynn scoffed. "God wasn't ready to take Jim home, that's all there is to it."

John nodded, but his curiosity got the better of him and he excused himself from the group.

"I'm going to take a little walk," he explained. "Be right back."

Diana watched him go, and knew where he was headed. She hoped Mrs. Robinson would be happy with the news of Jim's recovery.

Out in the corridor, John walked toward the front desk and asked what floor Thelma Robinson was on.

"She's on the third floor, sir," the receptionist said. "Room 316, in the observation unit."

John thanked the woman and rode the elevator to the third floor. There he approached the nurses' station and waited until someone noticed him.

"Can I help you, sir?" a woman asked. John glanced at the name on her badge and saw that she was the head nurse for that floor.

"Yes, ma'am, I'm looking for our neighbor, Mrs. Thelma Robinson. She's a friend of our family's. I understand she's in Room 316."

The nurse's eyes fell. "I'm sorry, sir," she said, unsure of whether she should tell him what had happened. "Mrs. Robinson passed away a few hours ago."

John felt his heart skip a beat as he stood frozen in place, stunned by the news. "But I thought she was only in for routine tests."

"That's right, sir, she was." The nurse lowered her clipboard and frowned. "Then a few hours ago her heart just stopped. We worked with her for some time trying to bring her back, but her body didn't respond.

"Again, I'm sorry to have to tell you this."

John thanked the nurse and turned back down the hallway to the elevator. He felt as though he were in a trance as he walked through the hospital to the waiting room on the first floor. When he entered the room, the others saw how strangely he looked and the room became quiet.

"What is it, John?" Lynn asked, worried that Jim might have taken another sudden turn for the worse.

"It's Mrs. Robinson, Dad." John's voice was flat, void of emotion. "She's dead. She died a few hours ago—about the same time Jim's body had begun making its comeback."

"That's impossible," Judy said, shaking her head as fresh tears sprung to her eyes. "Mrs. Robinson was only here for routine tests."

"The nurse told me her heart stopped," John added. "She went to sleep last night and died before she ever woke up."

The room grew silent again as each of them absorbed the amazing truth. Thelma Robinson had prayed for Jim to live, asking God to let her go in his place. Now that very thing had happened, and doctors had no explanation for either Jim's recovery or Thelma's death.

"Do you think what happened was an answer to her prayer?" John asked, looking incredulously at the other faces in the room.

For a moment no one spoke. Then Lynn sat up straighter and tilted his head thoughtfully.

"Well, son, I don't think there's one of us here who can discount the truth of what's happened these past few hours. Sure as I'm sitting here today, I'm convinced that Thelma returned to her room last night and asked God in all his mercy to take her home and let Jim live."

He looked at the others. "And sure enough, that's what happened." A smile came across his face.

"I guess it's like we were saying last night. The prayer of a righteous person is powerful and effective. Whatever we do, let's not forget that. Because that might just be all the explanation we'll ever get for what's just happened here."

Years later, long after Jim had recovered completely and returned home with his family, no one in the Christensen family ever forgot Thelma Robinson, her mysterious prayer, or what happened that night at the hospital in Marion, Kansas.